HOW TO DRAW SURREALIST ART
A CREATIVE DRAWING GUIDE FOR KIDS

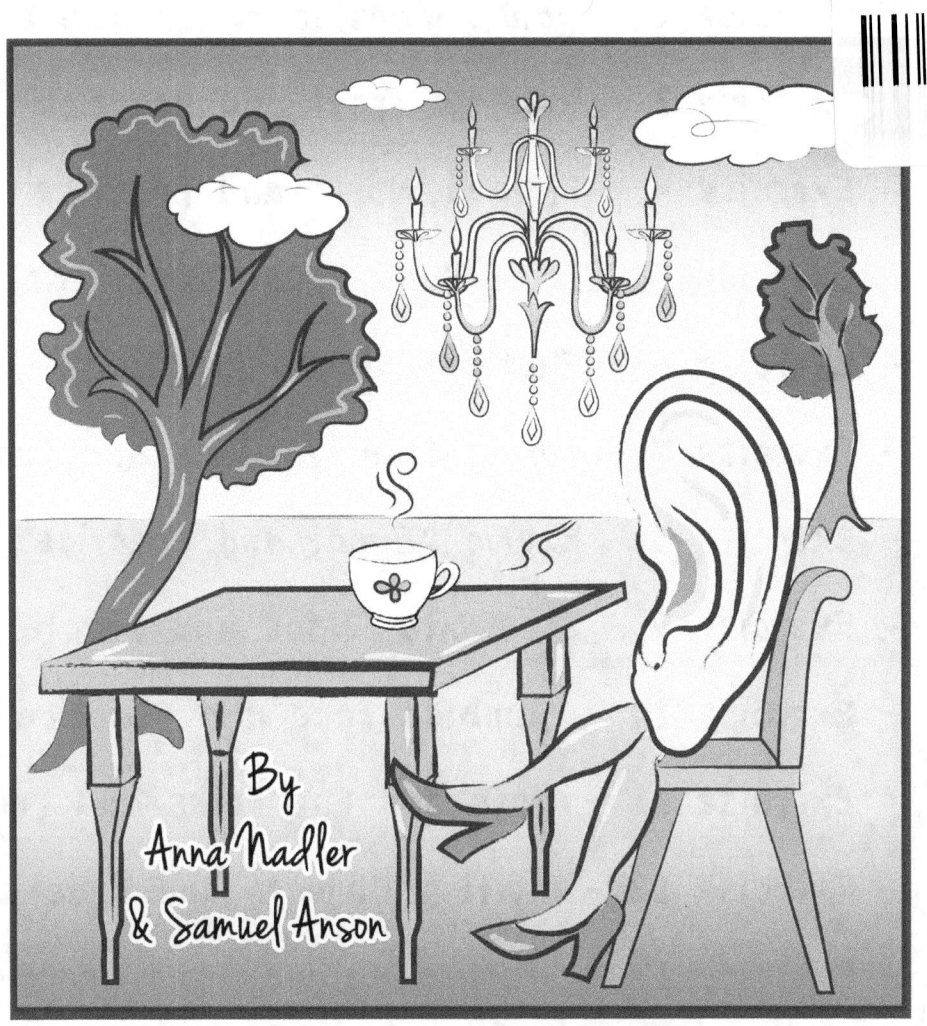

By Anna Nadler & Samuel Anson

Copyright © 2020 Anna Nadler
All rights reserved
Published by Little Birdie Press™
No part of this publication may be
reproduced, stored in a retrieval system or
transmitted in any form or by any means,
electronic, mechanical, photocopying, recording
or otherwise, without prior written permission
from the author/publisher.
www.annanadler.com

Table of Contents

p.4-5 - About the author

p.6-7 - Introduction

p.8-9 - Exercise 1 - Surreal Eye and Practice

p.10-11 - Exercise 2 - Hands Monster and Practice

p.12-13 - Exercise 3 - Role Reversal and Practice

p.14-15 - Exercise 4 - Flipped World and Practice

p.16-17 - Exercise 5 - Fruit Head People and Practice

p.18-19 - Exercise 6 - Exotic Bird and Practice

p.20-21 - Exercise 7 - Flying Chairs/Tables and Practice

p.22-23 - Exercise 8 - Exotic Animal and Practice

p.24-25 - Exercise 9 - Step into Space and Practice

p.26-27 - Exercise 10 - Jumbled Face and Practice

p.28-29 - Exercise 11 - Nose and Ear Folks and Practice

p.30-31 - Exercise 12 - Melting Objects and Practice

p.32-33 - Exercise 13 - Warped Hallway and Practice

p.34-35 - Exercise 14 - Super Stretchy People and Practice

p.36-37 - Exercise 15 - Bulging Eye People and Practice

p.38-39 - Exercise 16 - Playing With Proportions and Practice

p.40-41 - Exercise 17 - Room in a Sphere and Practice

Table of Contents

p.42-43 - Exercise 18 - Face-Object and Practice

p.44-45 - Exercise 19 - Warped Street and Practice

p.46-47 - Exercise 20 - Weird Locations and Practice

p.48-49 - Exercise 21 - Fantastical Animals and Practice

p.50-51 - Exercise 22 - Flower Hair and Practice

p.52-53 - Exercise 23 - Cat and Human Hybrid and Practice

p.54-55 - Exercise 24 - Living Room Outdoors and Practice

p.56-57 - Exercise 25 - Creepy Spider and Practice

p.58-59 - Exercise 26 - Face made of Fruit and Practice

p.60-61 - Exercise 27 - Shoe House and Practice

p.62-63 - Exercise 28 - Man with a Hole and Practice

p.64-65 - Exercise 29 - Jumbled Body and Practice

p.66-67 - Exercise 30 - Tree Person and Practice

p.68-69 - Final Note

p.70-100 - Drawing Practice Pages

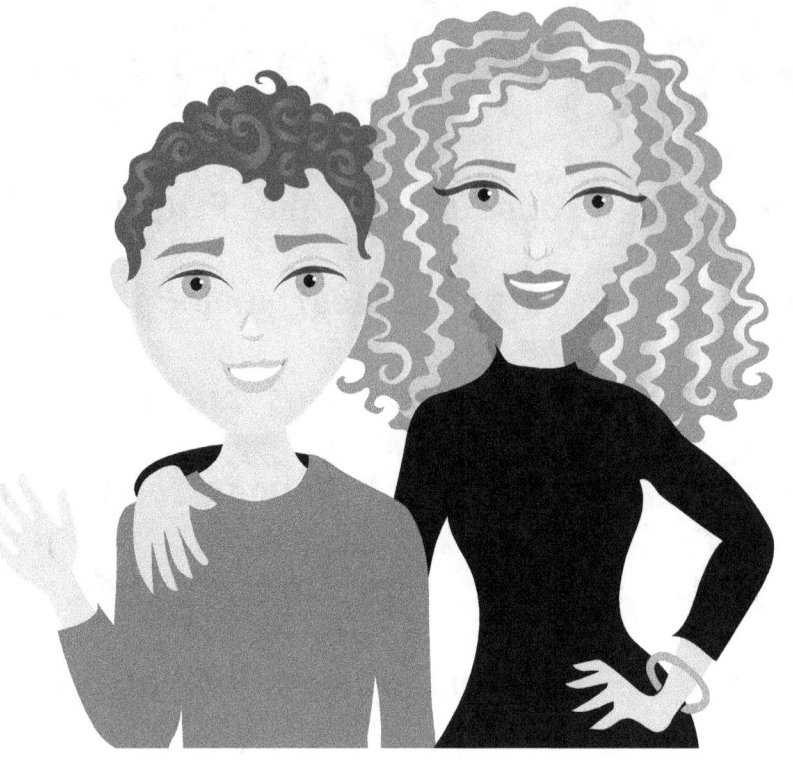

Anna Nadler is a book illustrator who lives and works in New York City. She has been drawing since the age of two - it's been her life-long passion and career for several decades. Anna has taught both kids and adults how to draw, and has finally decided to put some of that knowledge into a series of comprehensive books - for everyone to benefit.
This particular book was inspired by her very imaginative and creative son, Samuel Anson, who has also contributed fun ideas to it.

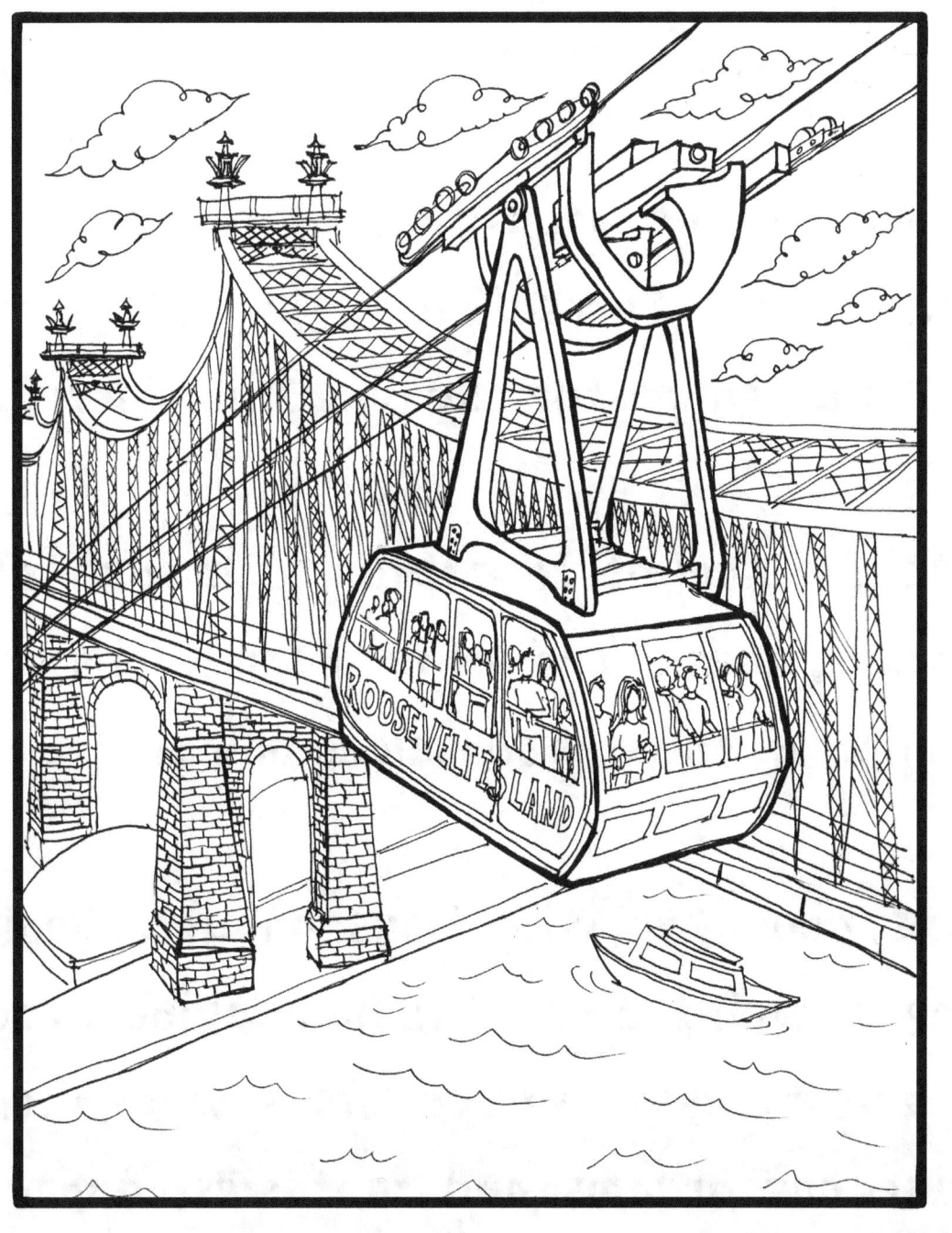

Anna Nadler loves to draw people, places, cities, animals, architecture, landscapes and travel sites. The more unique and interesting, the better.

You can find many of her original art books by searching her name on Amazon.

Dear Artist,

Welcome to this book on how to draw surrealist art! Surrealism is an art movement which started in the early 20th century.

Surrealists sought to capture, through art, literature, music and other forms, the inner workings of the subconscious mind.

In this book, we will focus on art. Imagine having a weird dream, then imagine drawing that dream. Many surrealists saw it their job to take our dreams and fantasies, and to turn them into creative and bizarre images for us to behold. These images would often be strange, irrational, sometimes even disturbing. But what they were not, they certainly were not boring.

Surrealism essentially takes ordinary everyday objects, and through unusual juxtaposition, proportion, scale, distortion, perspective and other tools, changes the objects to appear out of the ordinary, fantastical, odd, misshapen. It makes you question the laws of physics, laws of art, laws of nature...

Drawing in a surrealist style is a great exercise for your creativity. So, in this book, you will find 30 exercises to inspire your inner surrealist. You are going to make interesting, expressive, and engaging drawings that will encourage great creativity and captivate the viewer.

So, let's draw surrealist art!

Exercise 1

Ordinary eye: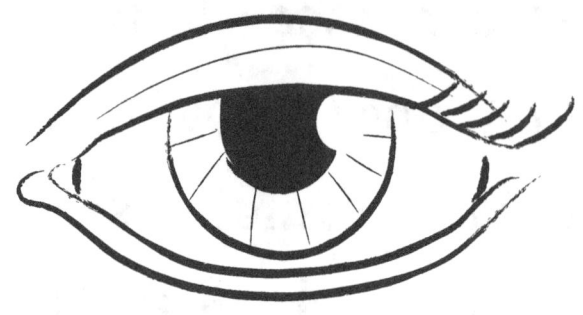

Surreal eye:

Let us add some interesting objects to our eye.

We can include a cityscape inside of our eye.
Or a body silhouette, for example.
This makes our eye drawing unusual and interesting.
You can use white pencil or pen on top of the dark.

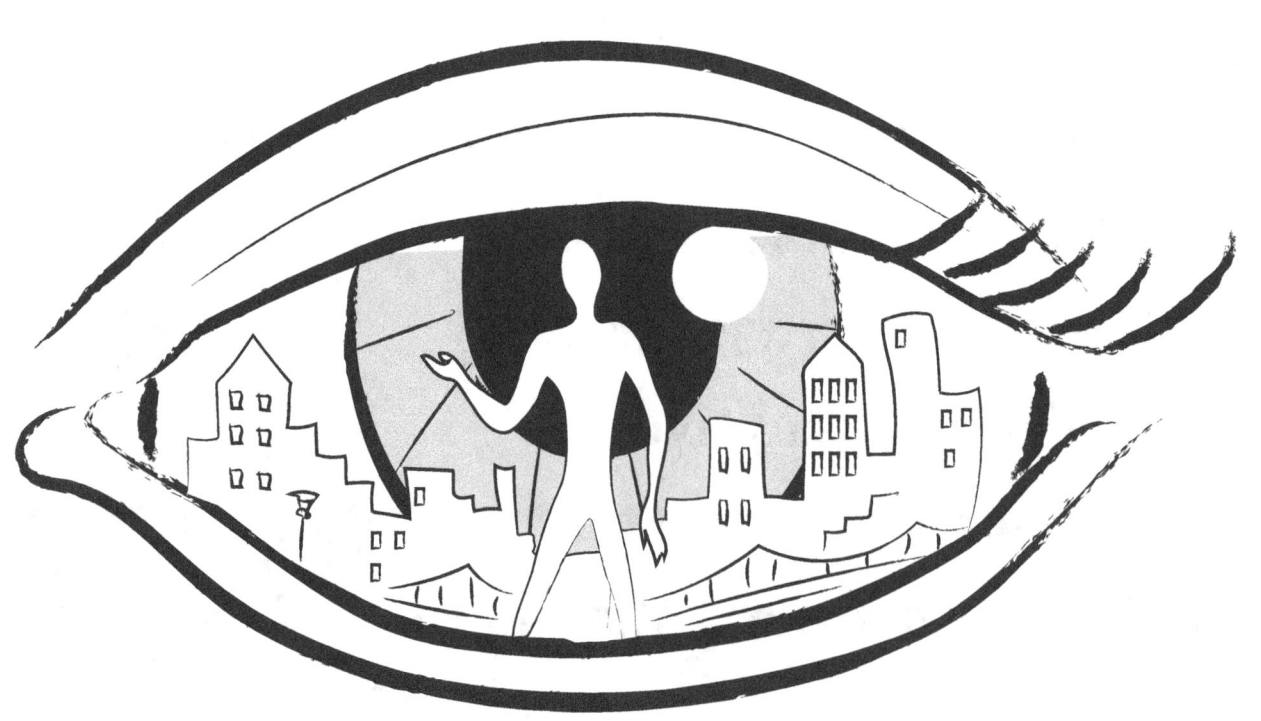

Surreal Eye Practice

Now you can make your own drawing of a surrealist style eye. Draw a regular eye with a pencil, then erase a part and draw in a city scape with a person in the foreground. When you are done, you can outline the drawing with black maker or pens of different thicknesses.

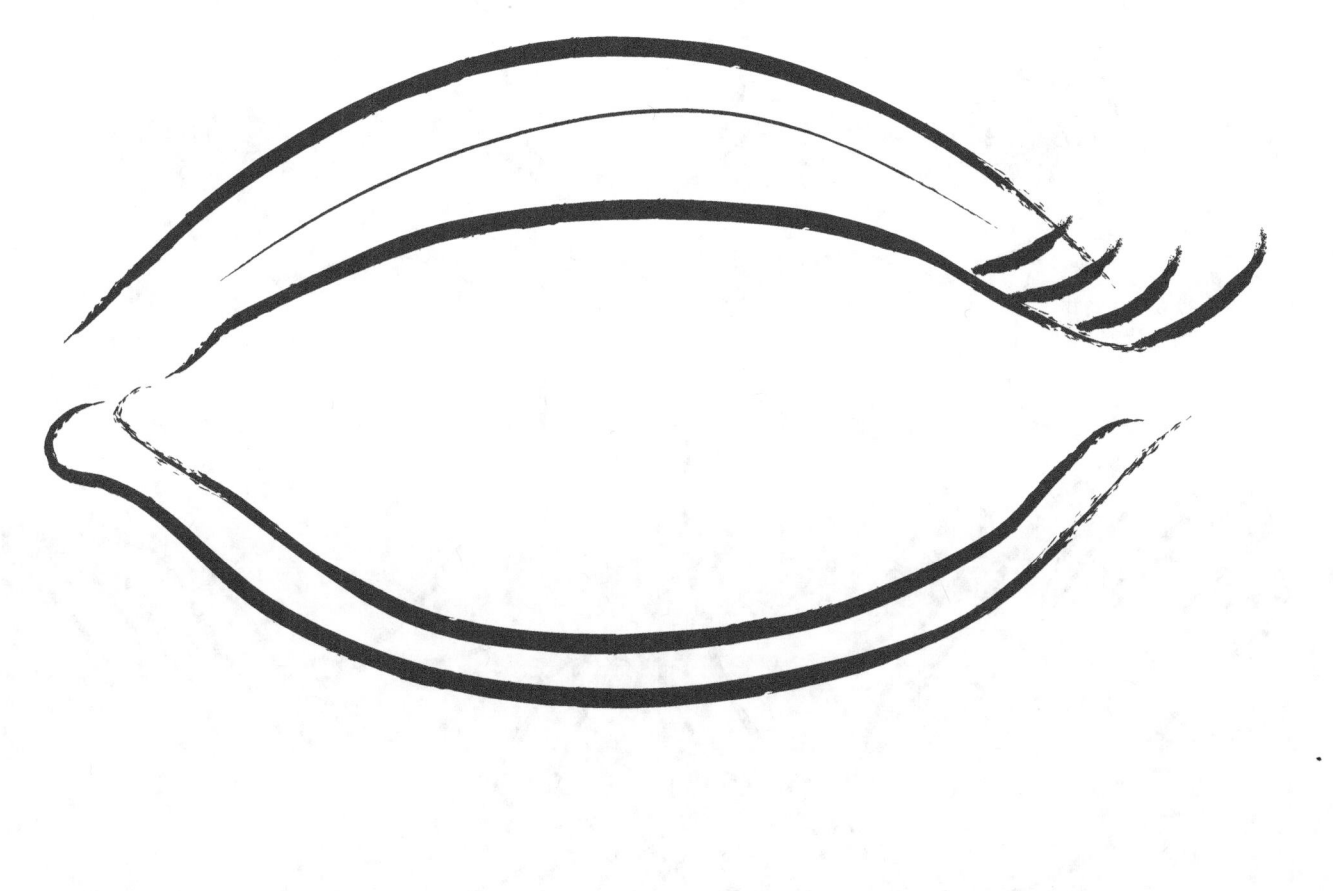

Exercise 2   Hands monster

In this exercise we will create a monster made of hands. We can add small details such as eyeballs, to make it more clear that it's a monster.

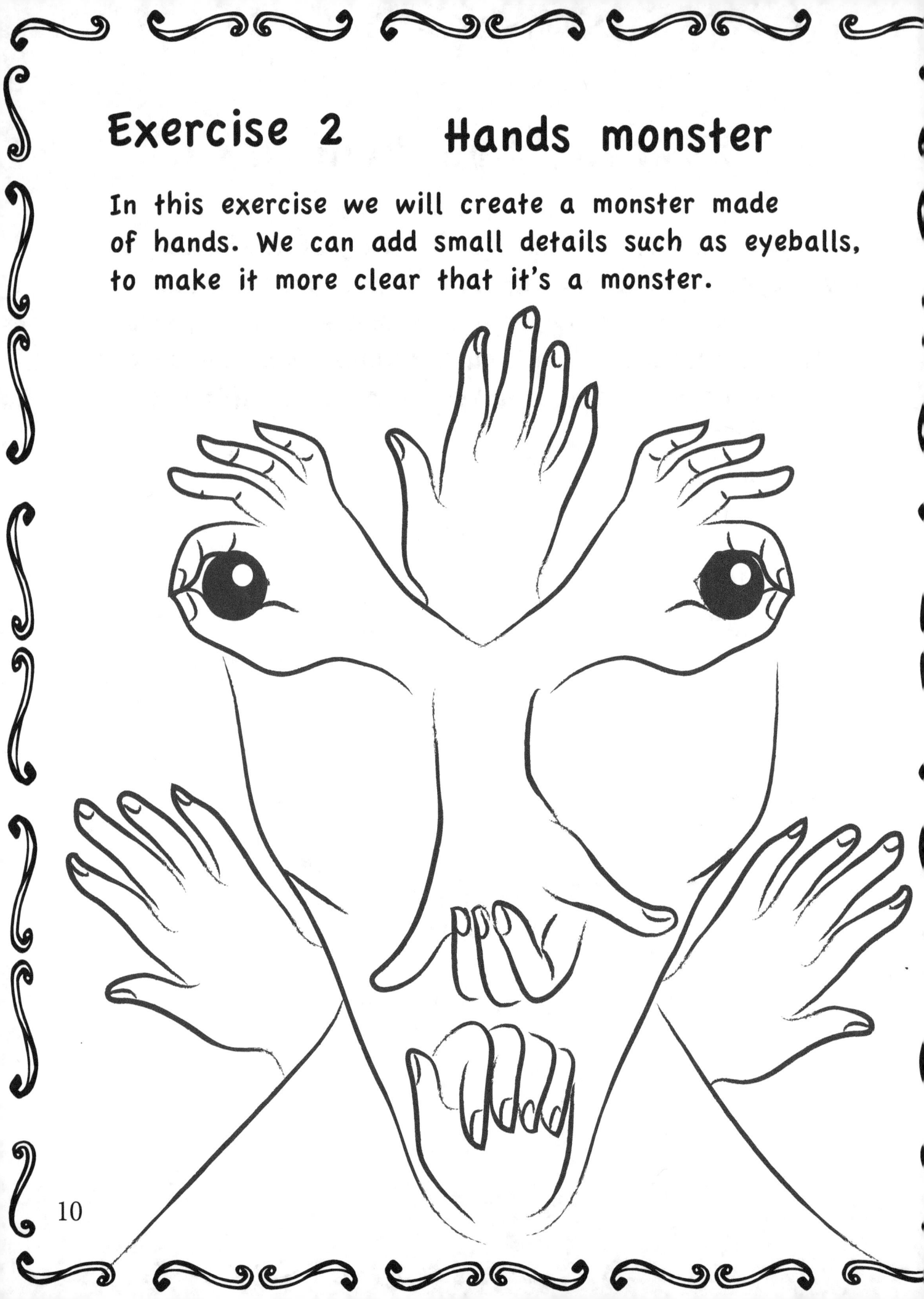

Hands Monster Practice

Using the hands shown below, try to create a "monster." You can make it symmetrical to make it clear and add eye balls or other details to your monster. You can also use your own hand positions, which aren't shown here. Look at your own hands and try to draw them, then use those drawings to combine them into a unique "monster."

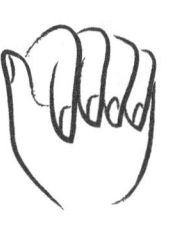 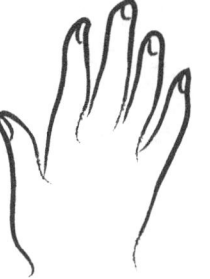 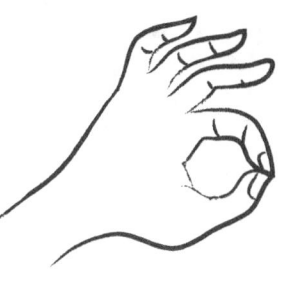 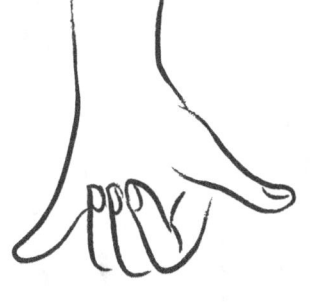

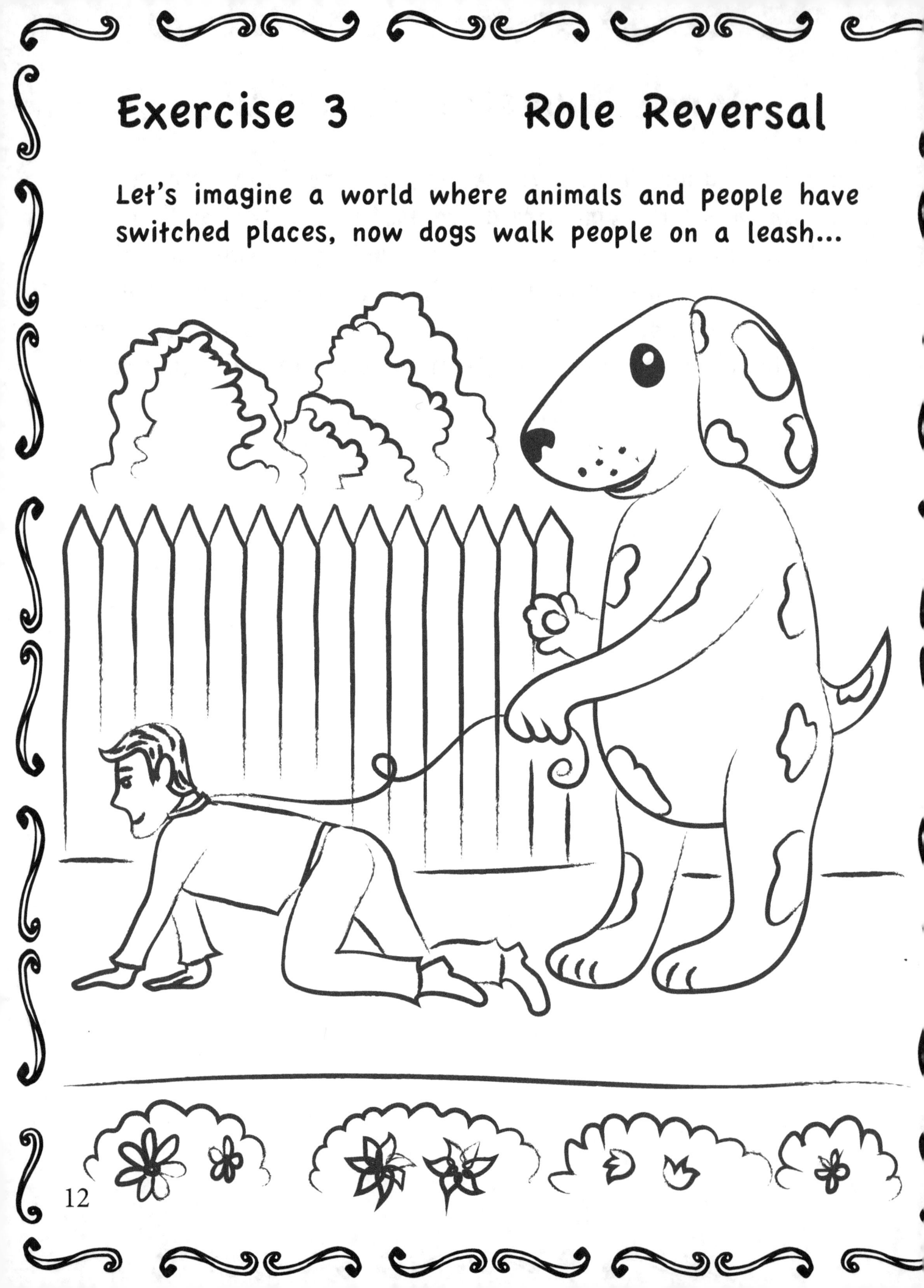

Role Reversal Practice

Now try this, if you have any pets, draw them life, human size. Then draw yourself the size of the pet. You can have them walk you on a leash or playing. Let your imagination soar! Use the scene to place your pet and yourself there.

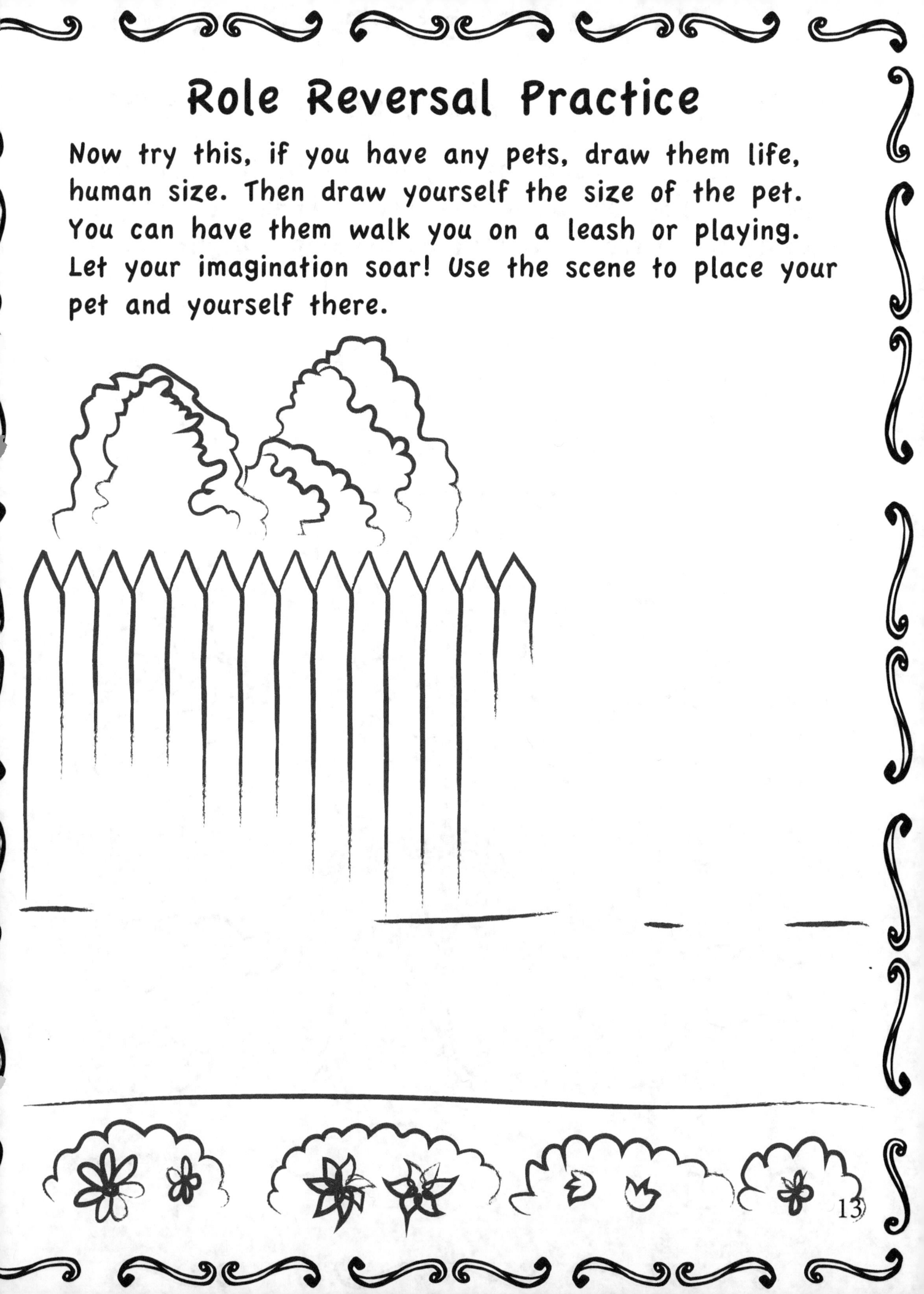

Exercise 4   The world - flipped

In this exercise make the sky at the bottom and the ground at the top, as if you were standing on your head. Except, our person will still be walking upright.

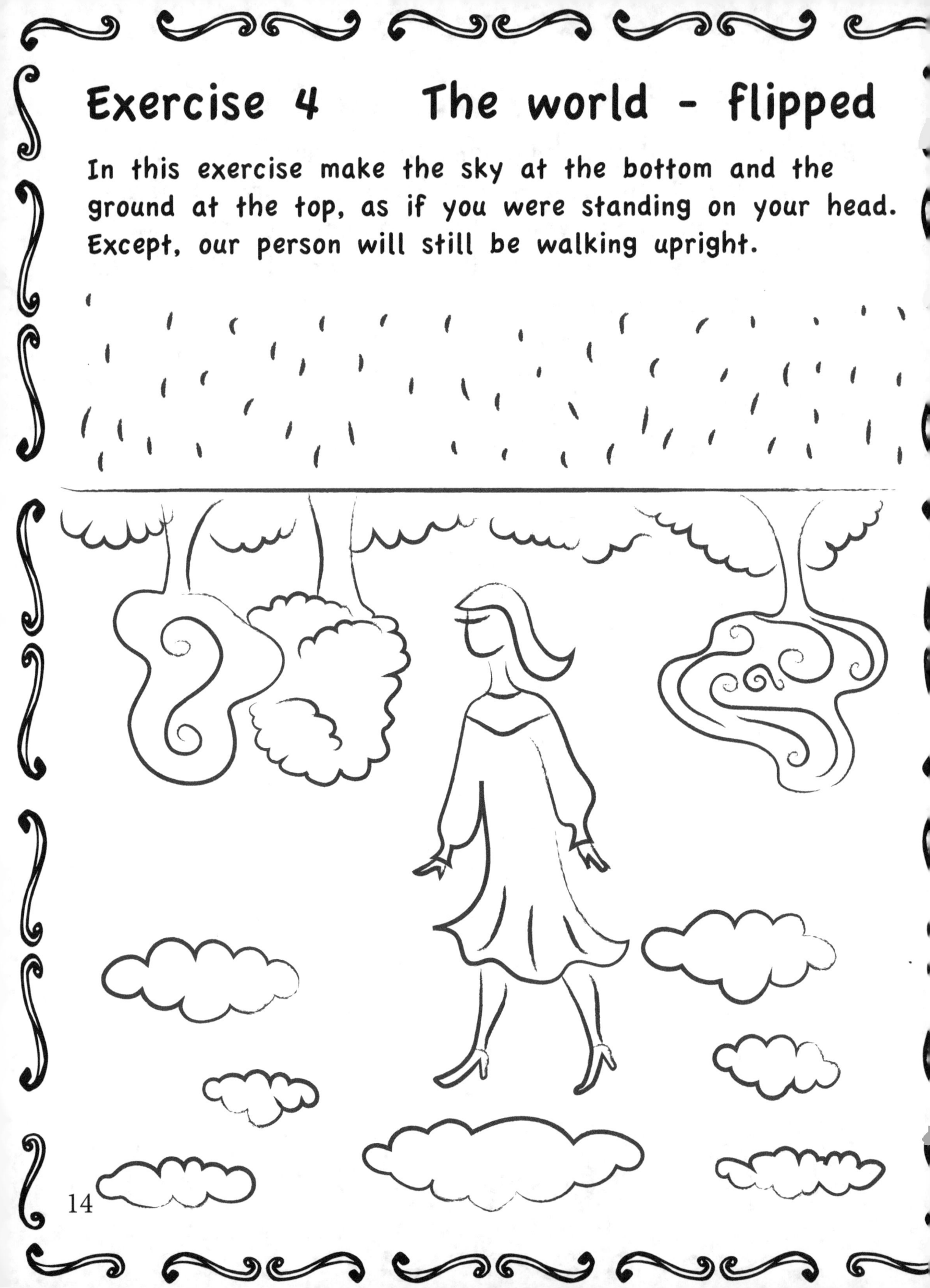

Flipped World - Practice

Now you can create a simple drawing of outdoors, with it being flipped. Draw a simple person walking on the sky/clouds. You can flip the page, if it is easier for you to draw the world upright first. Then you can flip it again and draw the person. Make sure to leave room for the person in the picture.

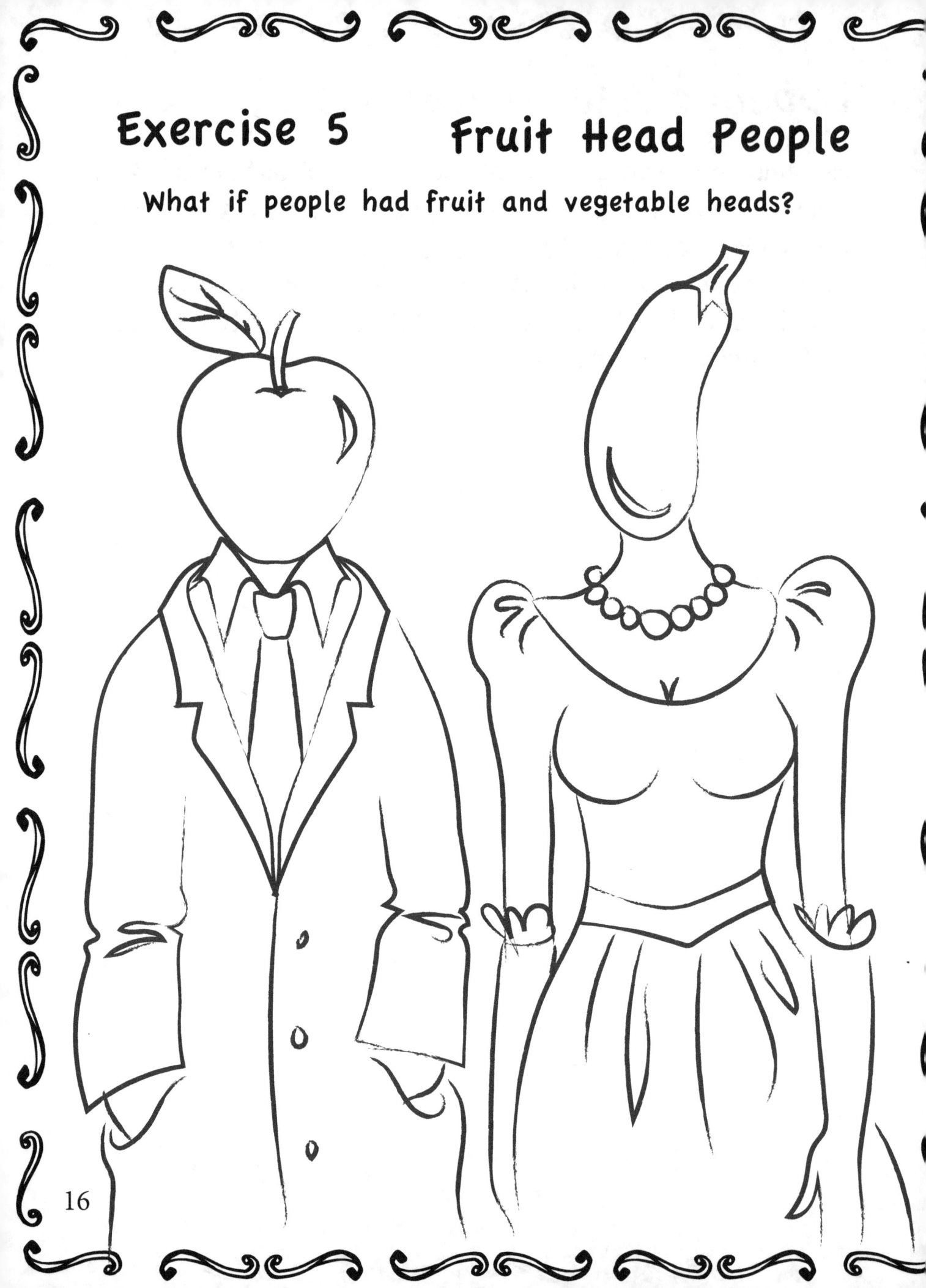

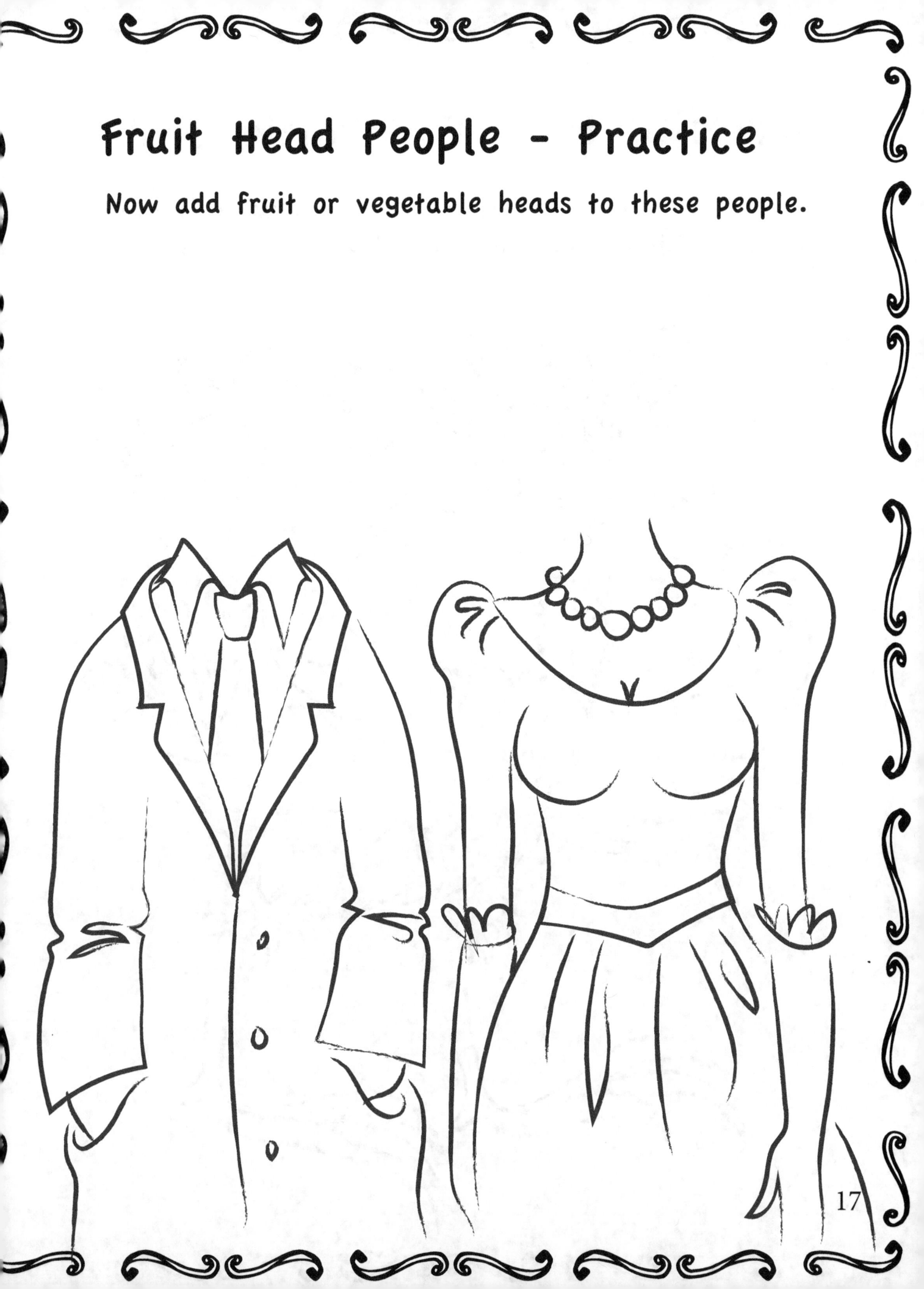

Exercise 6 — Exotic bird

In this exercise, we will combine several different kinds of birds into one exotic flying creature.

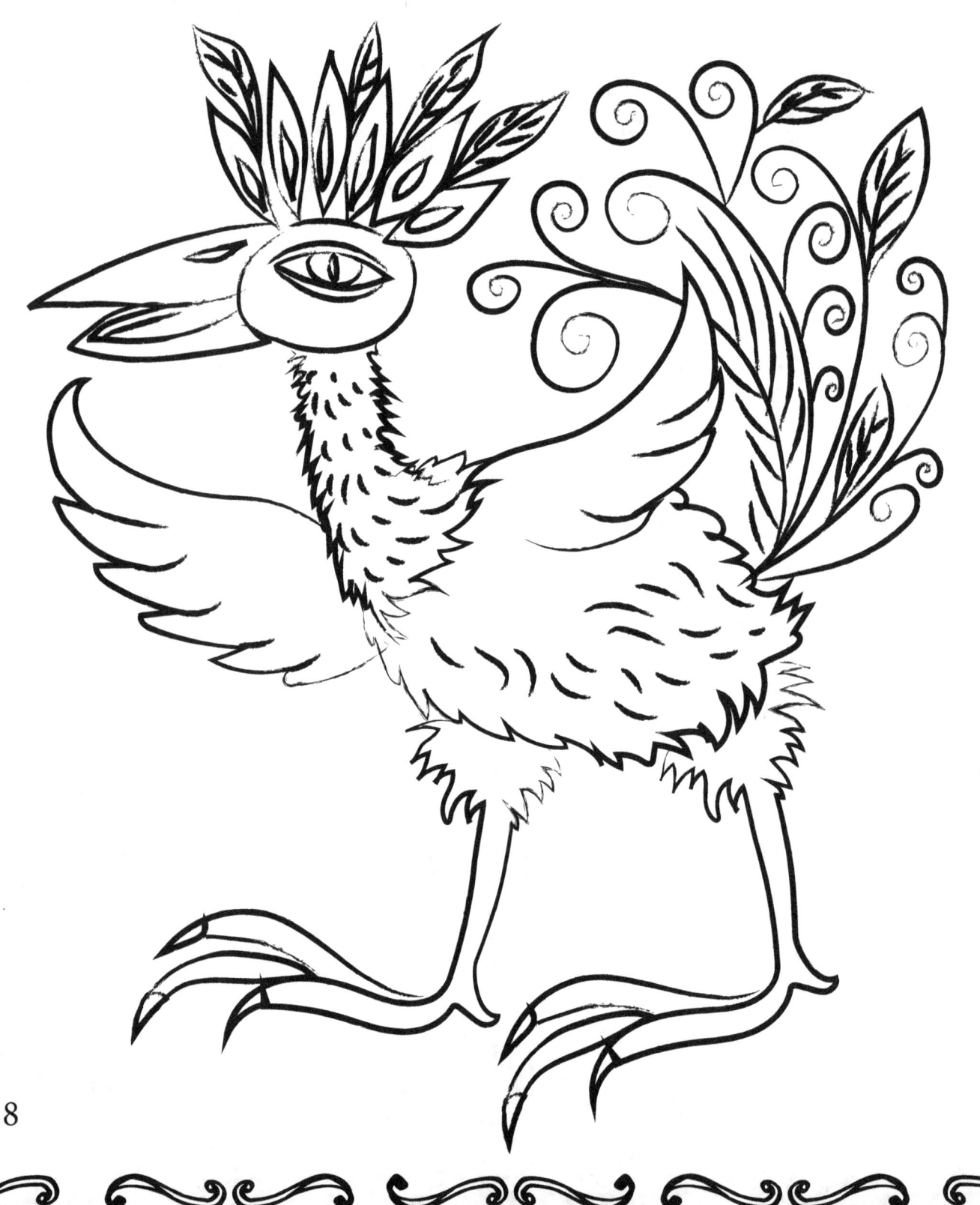

Exotic bird - Practice

Now use elements of different birds to make your exotic bird. You can use some of these or come up with your own.

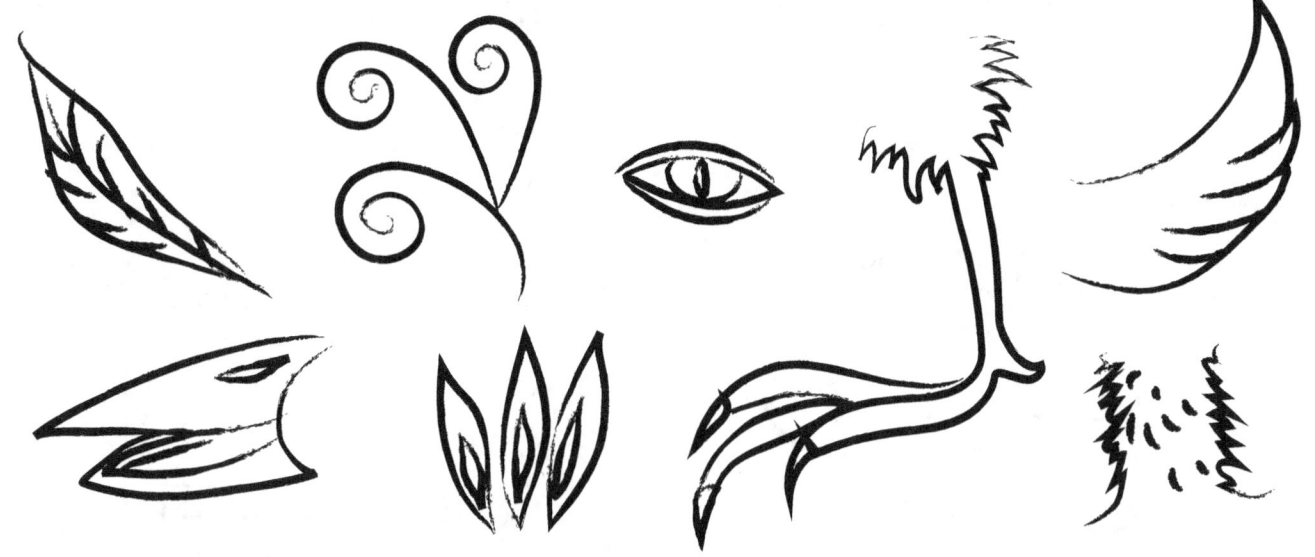

Exercise 7
Chairs and tables can fly

In this exercise let's make our chairs float up in the sky!

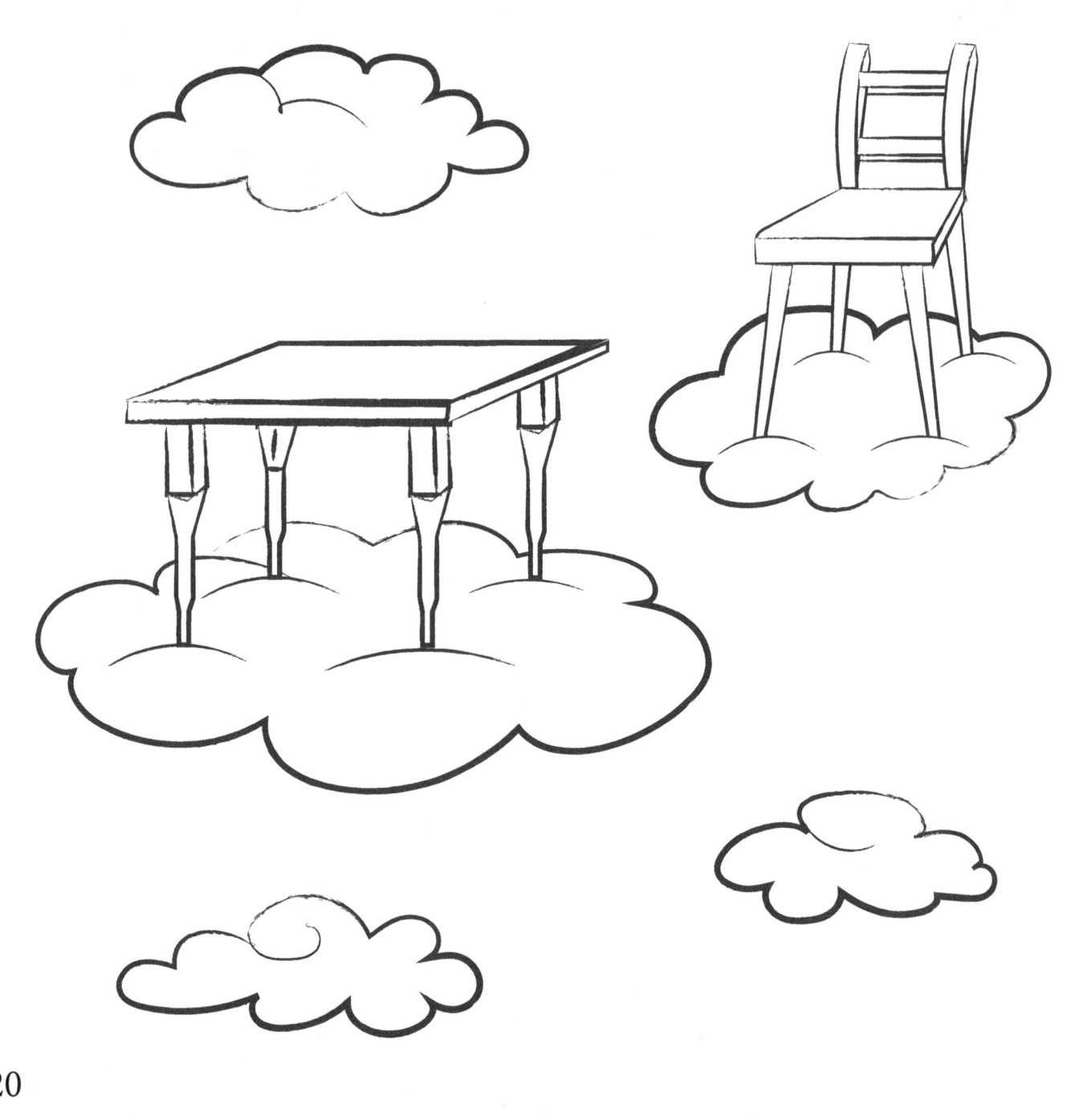

Chairs and tables can fly

Practice   Now add furniture to the clouds.

21

Exercise 8   Exotic animal

In this exercise, we will combine several different animals into one hybrid animal.

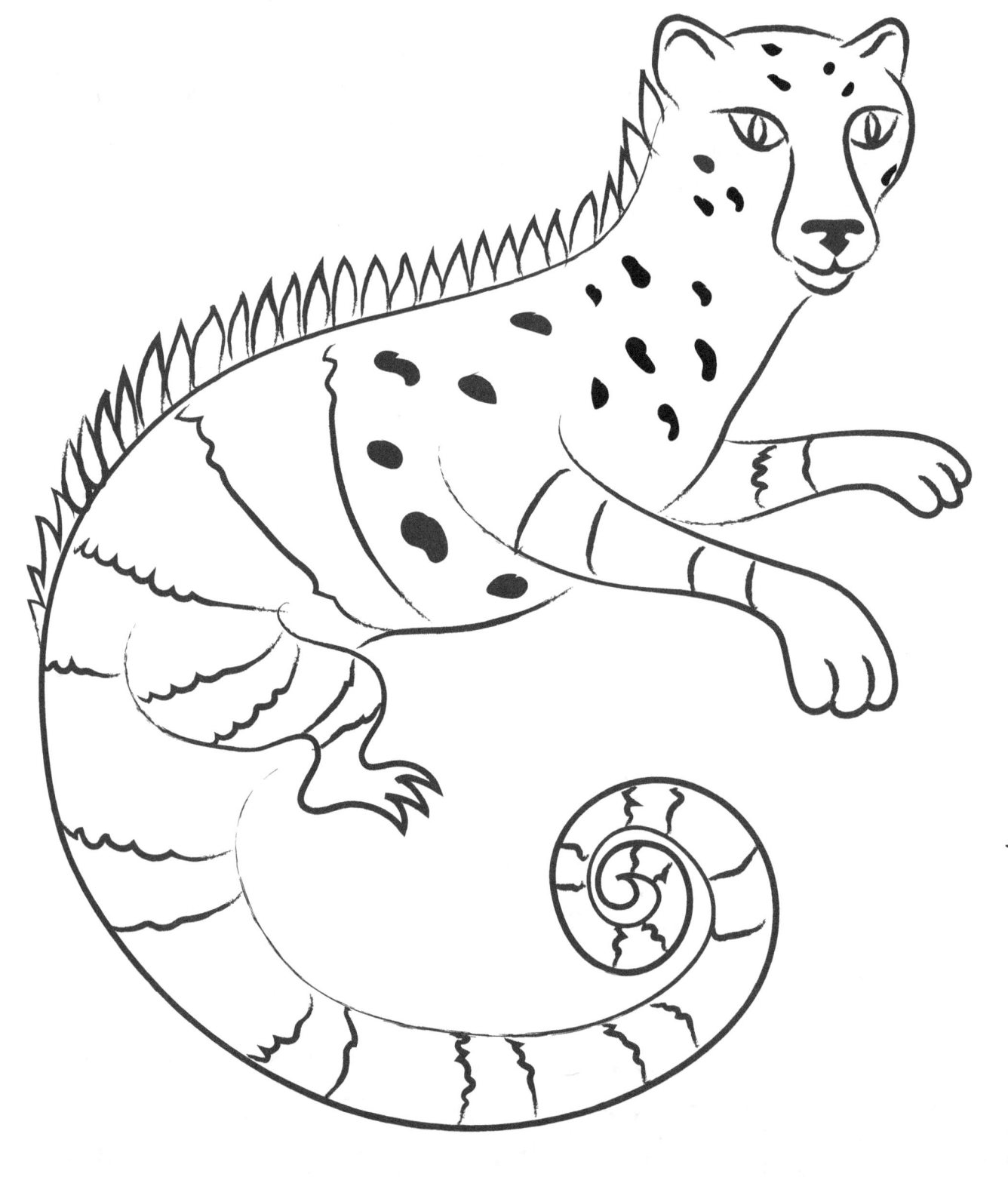

Exotic animal - Practice

Now let us combine parts of different animals to make one hybrid animal. You can use elements of tigers, chameleons, elephants, giraffes, and more!

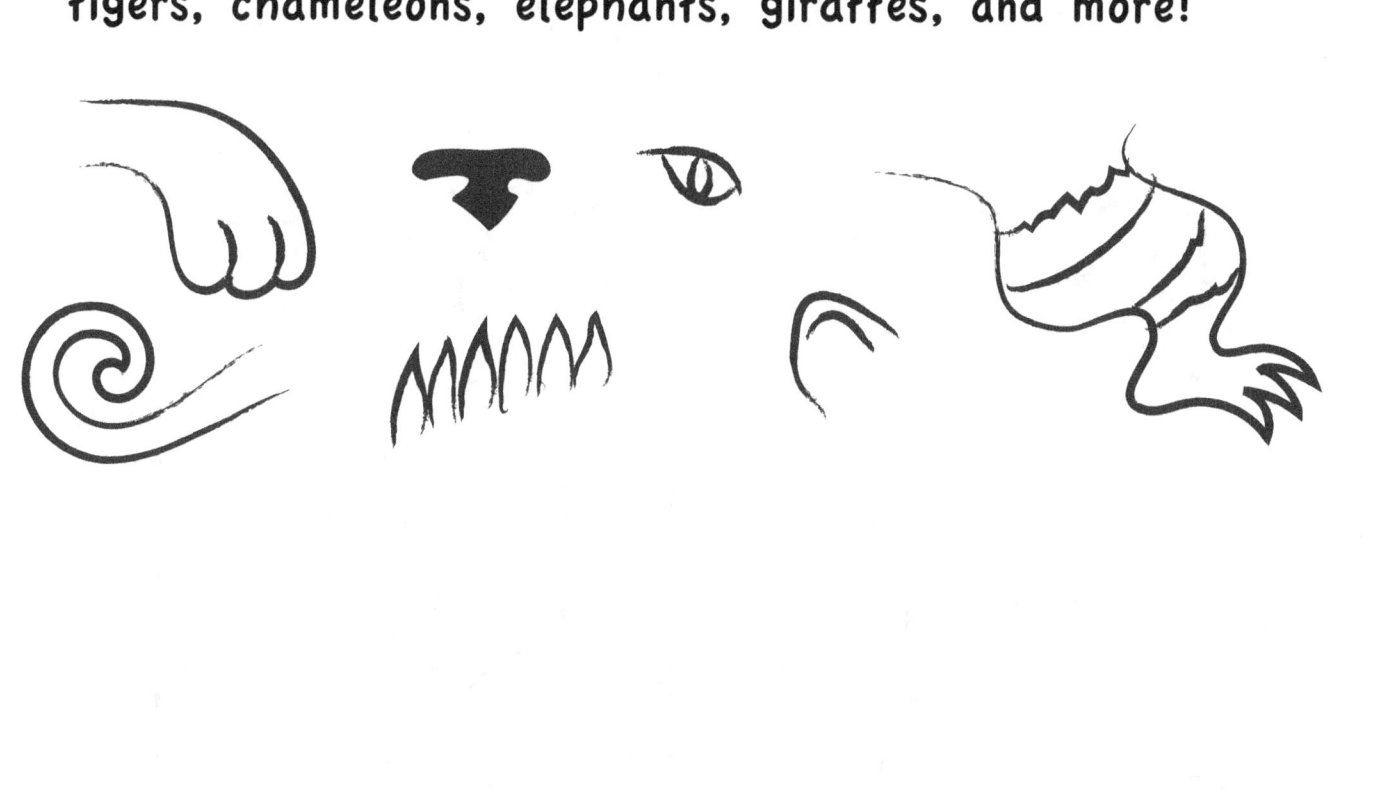

Exercise 9   Step into space

In this exercise let's draw a door into space! Step into a galaxy in your drawing! In the foreground, let us draw a partial closeup view of a planet.

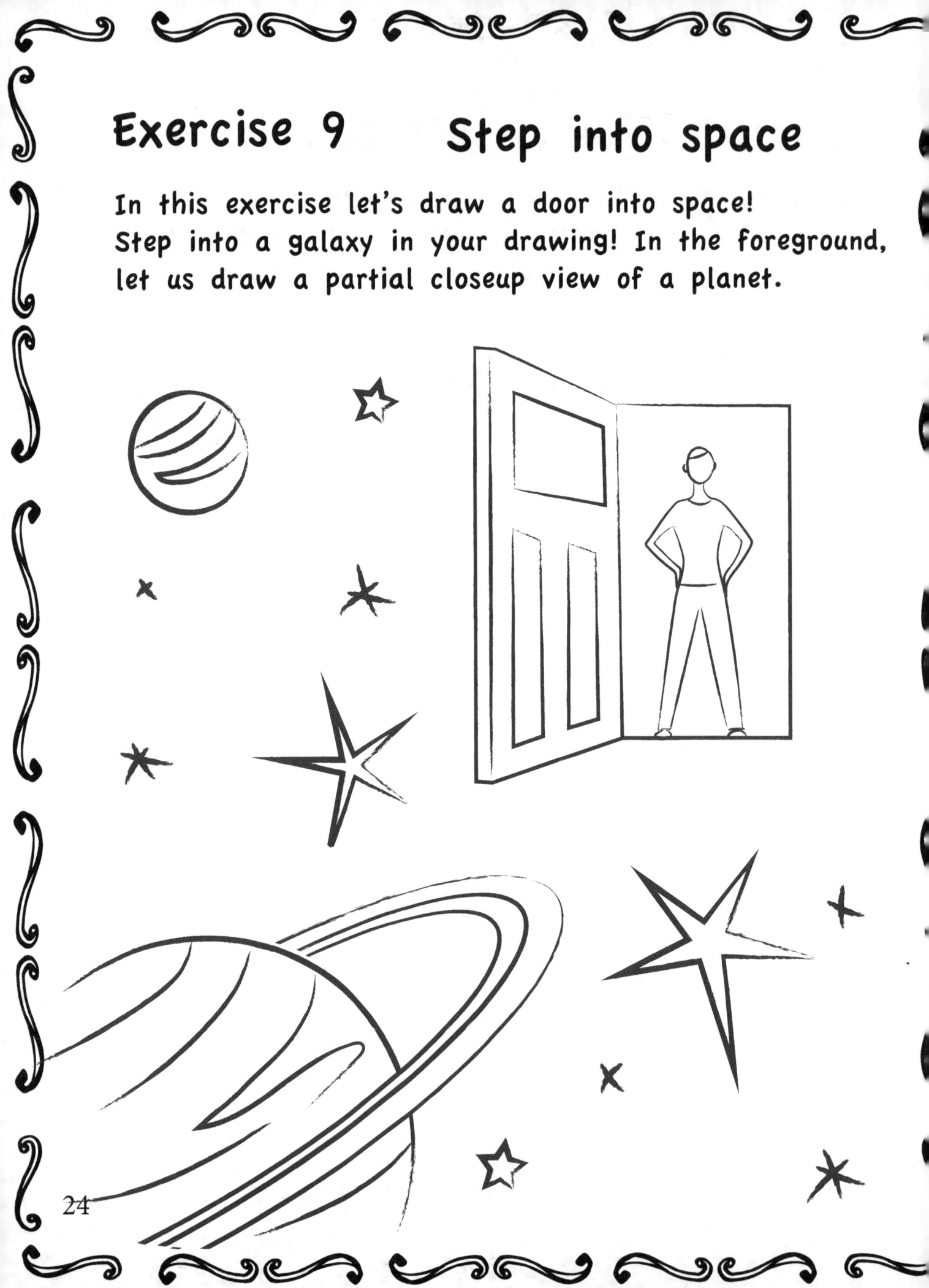

Step into space - practice

Now draw a person standing at the open door into space. Draw in planets, stars, and other cosmic objects.

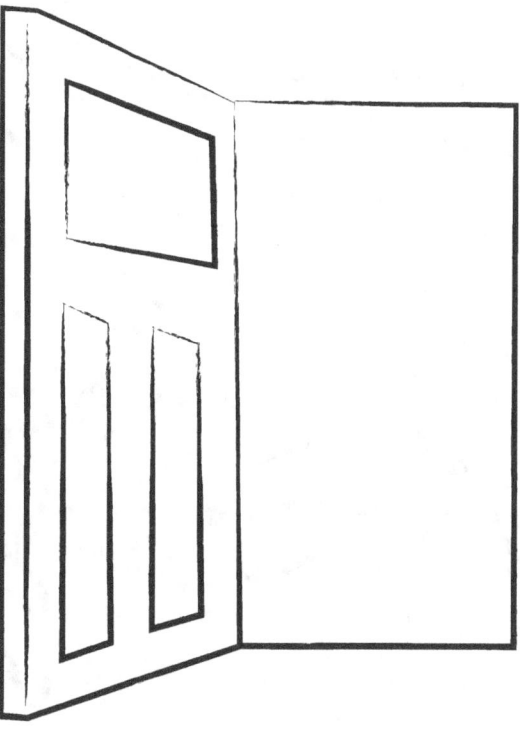

Exercise 10   Jumbled Face

In this exercise let us create a face with features which do not follow any rules, they can be placed in random places and be in different than normal numbers.

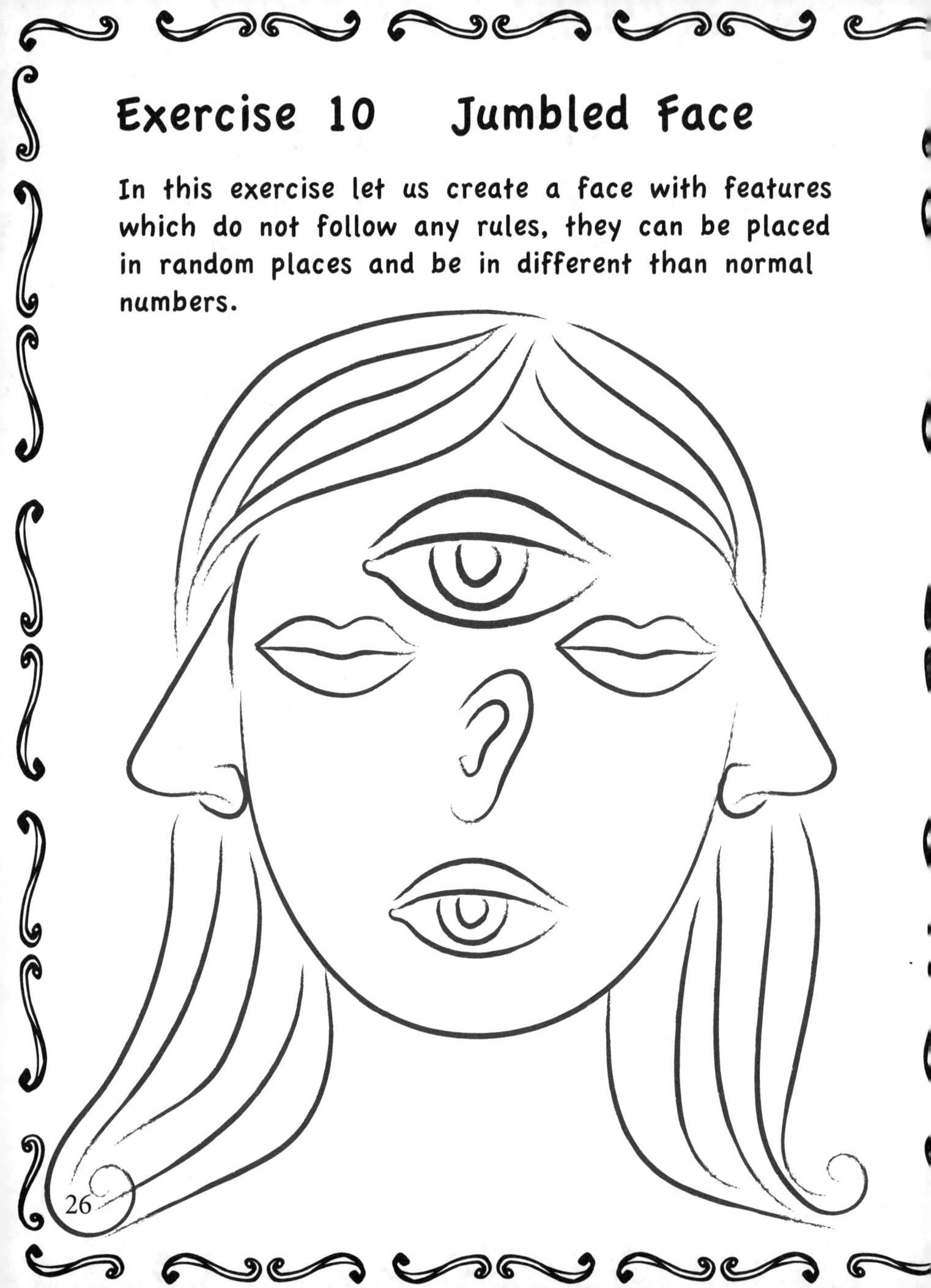

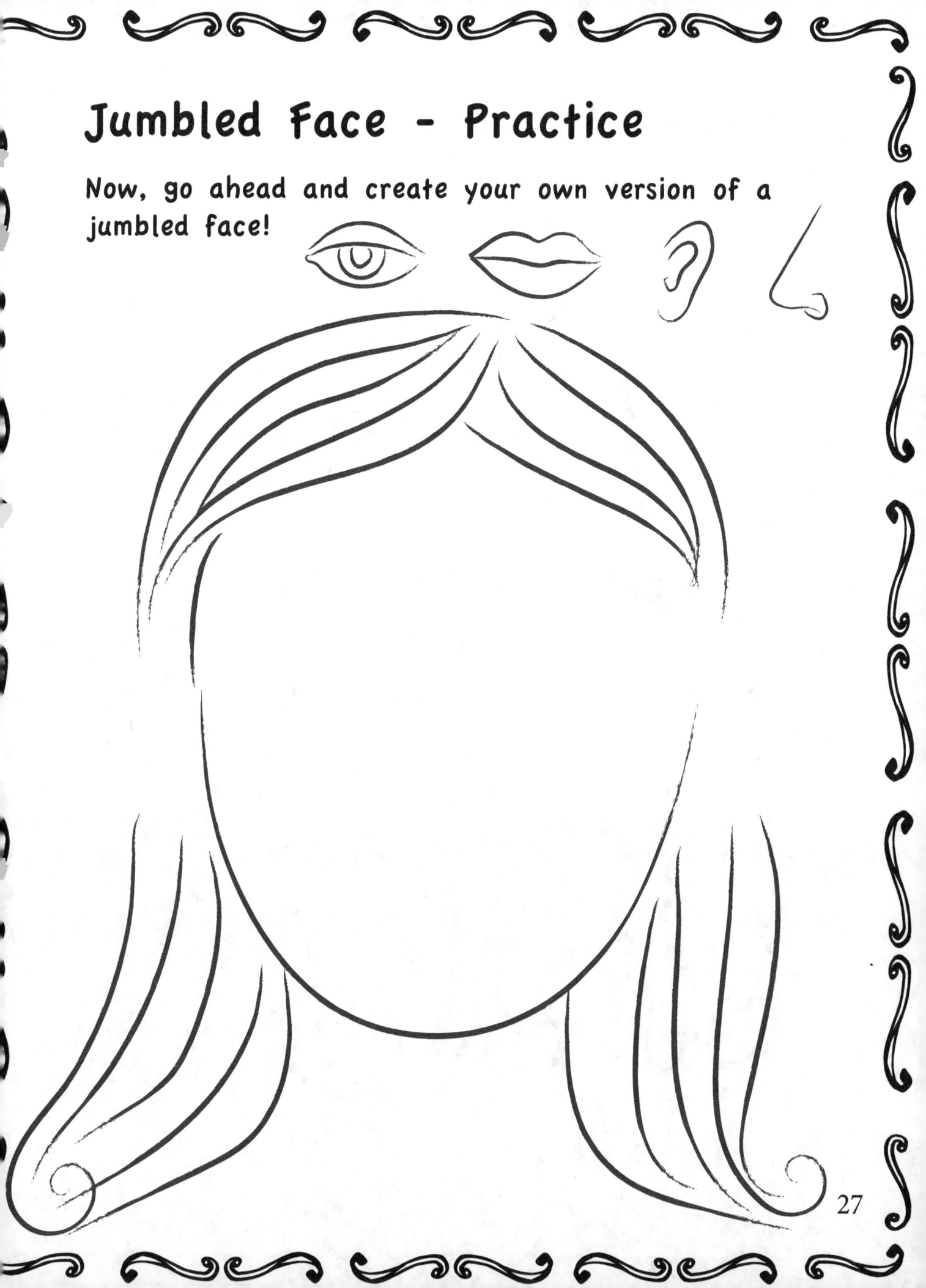

Exercise 11 Nose and Ear Folks

Now let us make cute people that are ear and nose people!

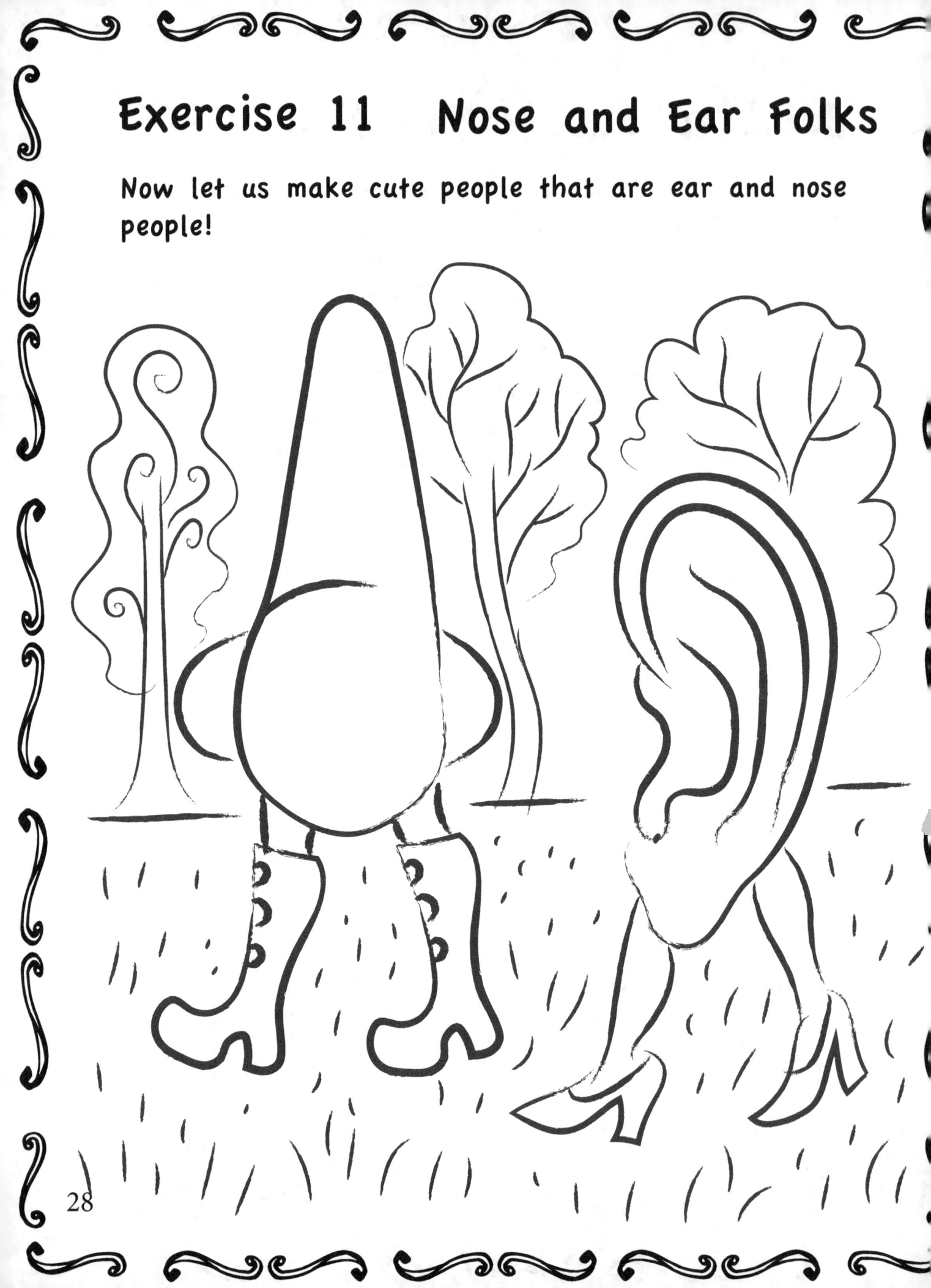

28

Nose and Ear Folks - Practice

Here you can practice adding feet and a background to the nose and ear people.

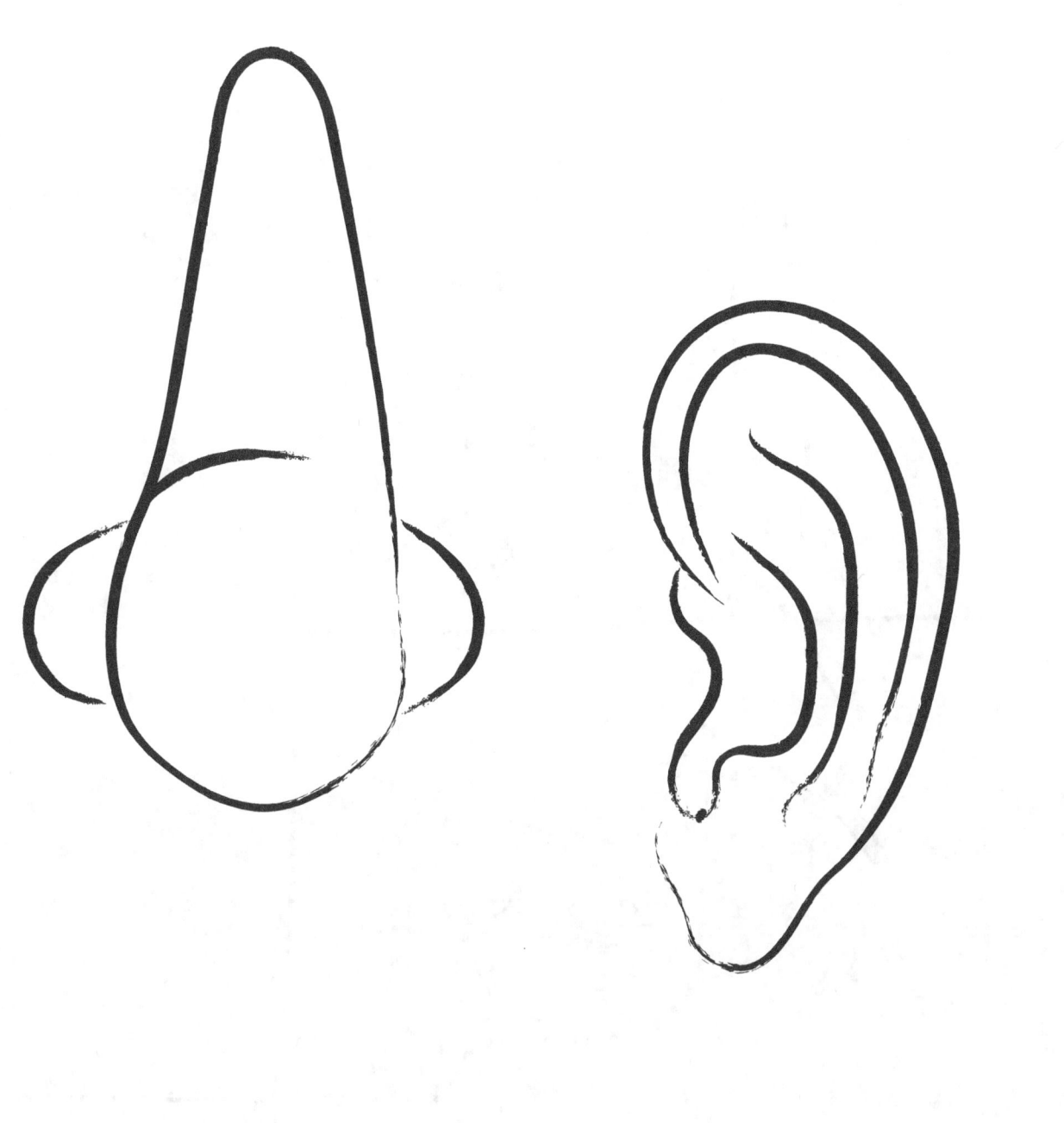

29

Exercise 12   Melting objects

Like the famous surrealist artist, Salvador Dali, here we can experiment with melting clocks.

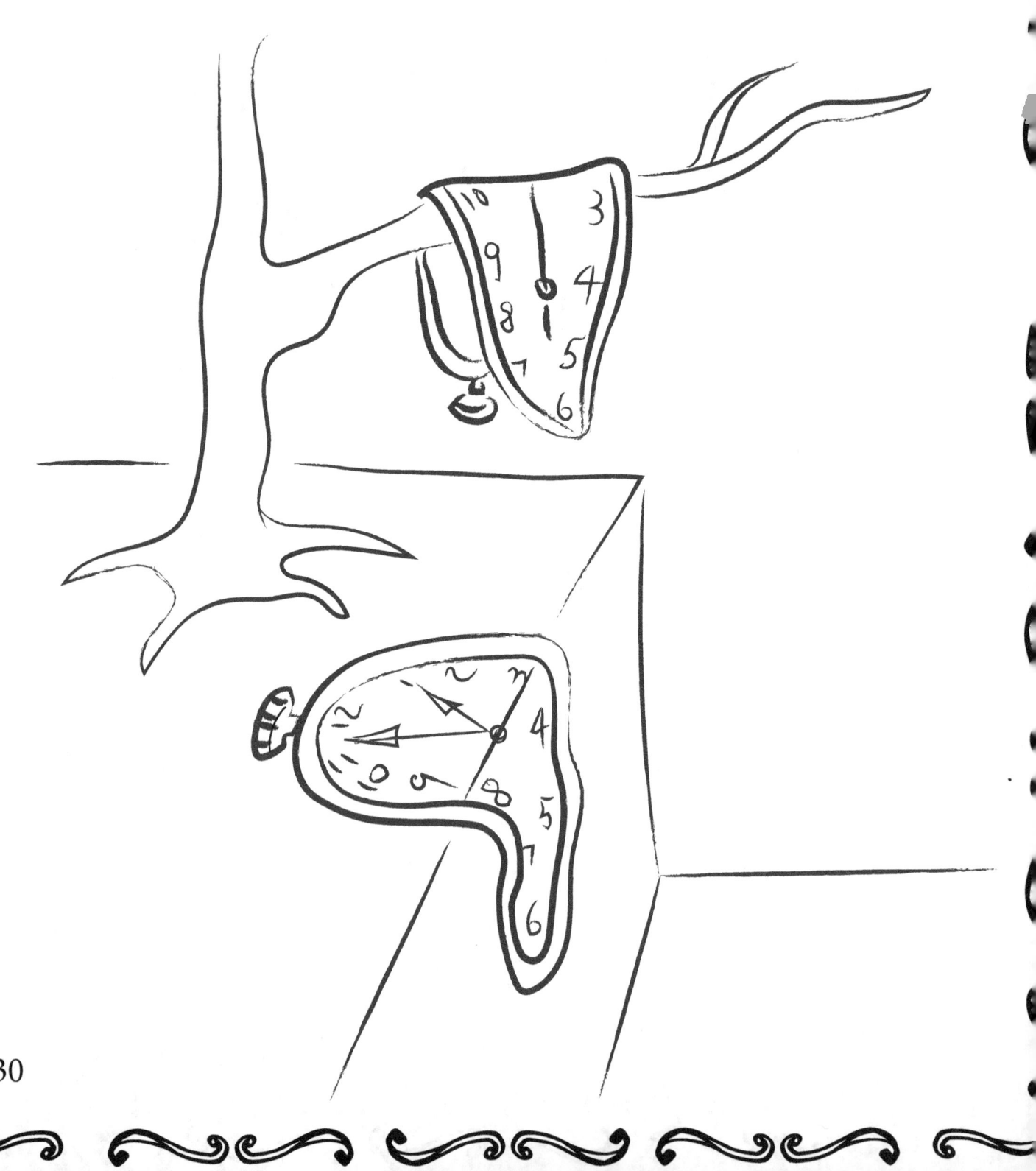

Melting objects - Practice

Now try to draw the melting clocks yourself. Refer to the drawings on the opposite page.

31

Exercise 13   Warped Hallway

Sometimes hallways get warped! How would it look if a hallway got distorted?

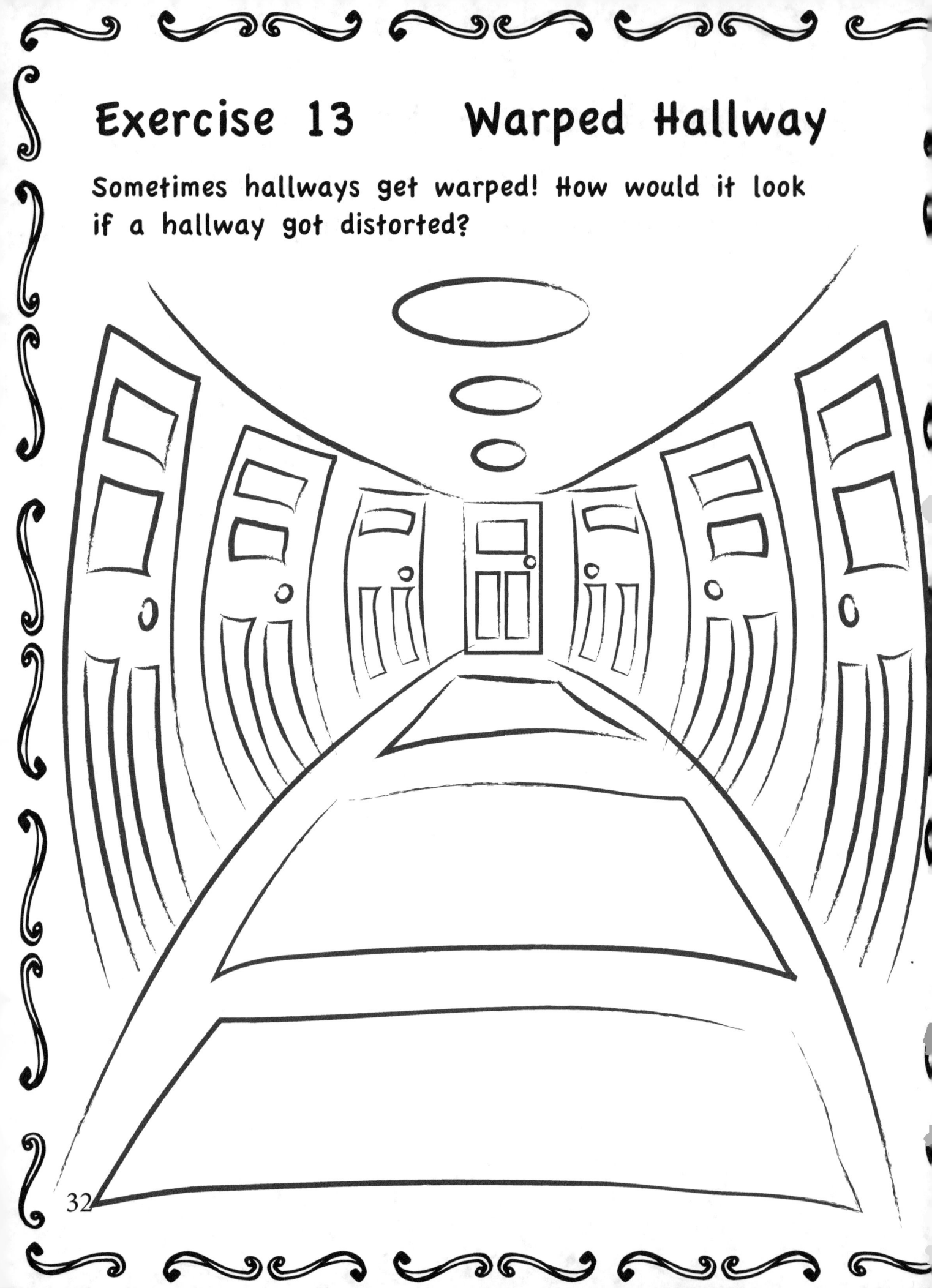

Warped Hallway - Practice

Now you can practice adding doors to your warped hallway, as you see on the opposite page.

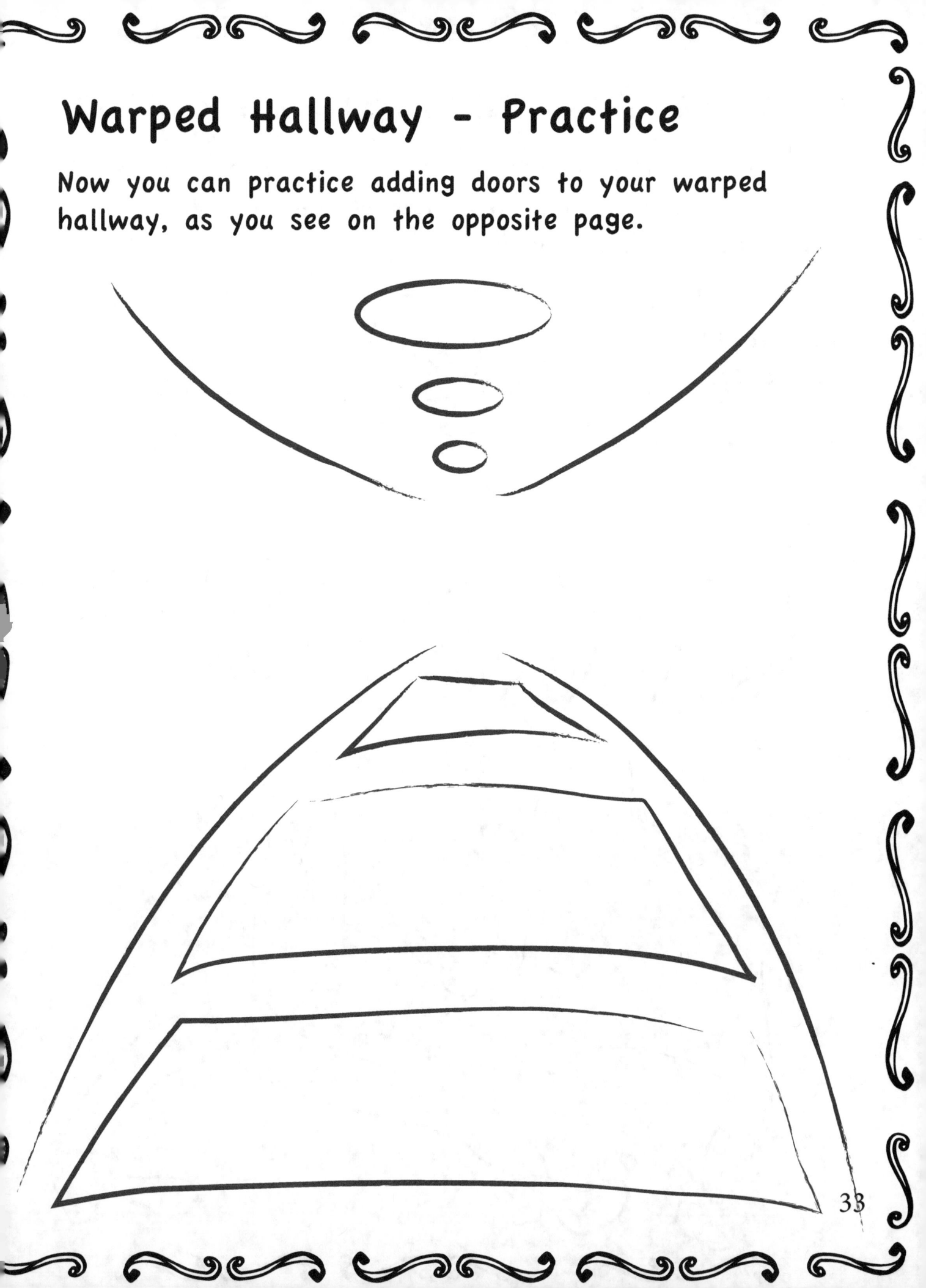

33

Exercise 14 Super Stretchy People

There are regular people and then there are super flexible people! Practice defying the laws of anatomy and biology with these stretchy folks!

Don't be afraid to make it very exaggerated!

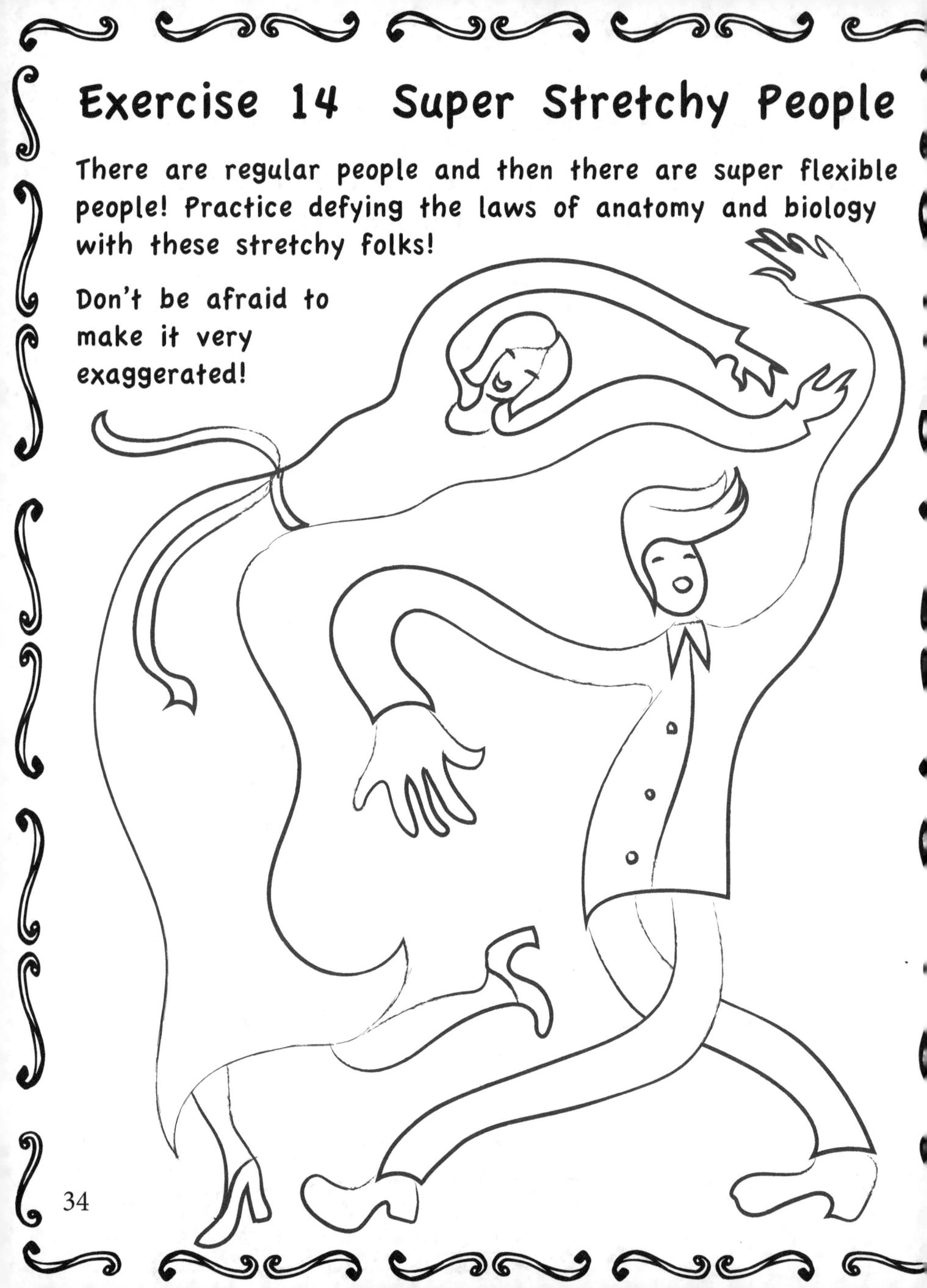

Super Stretchy People - Practice

Many of these exercises are designed to help you make more expressive drawings. This is certainly one of them! Connect the body parts in a fun way - to make your own super stretchy people! You can even overlap them!

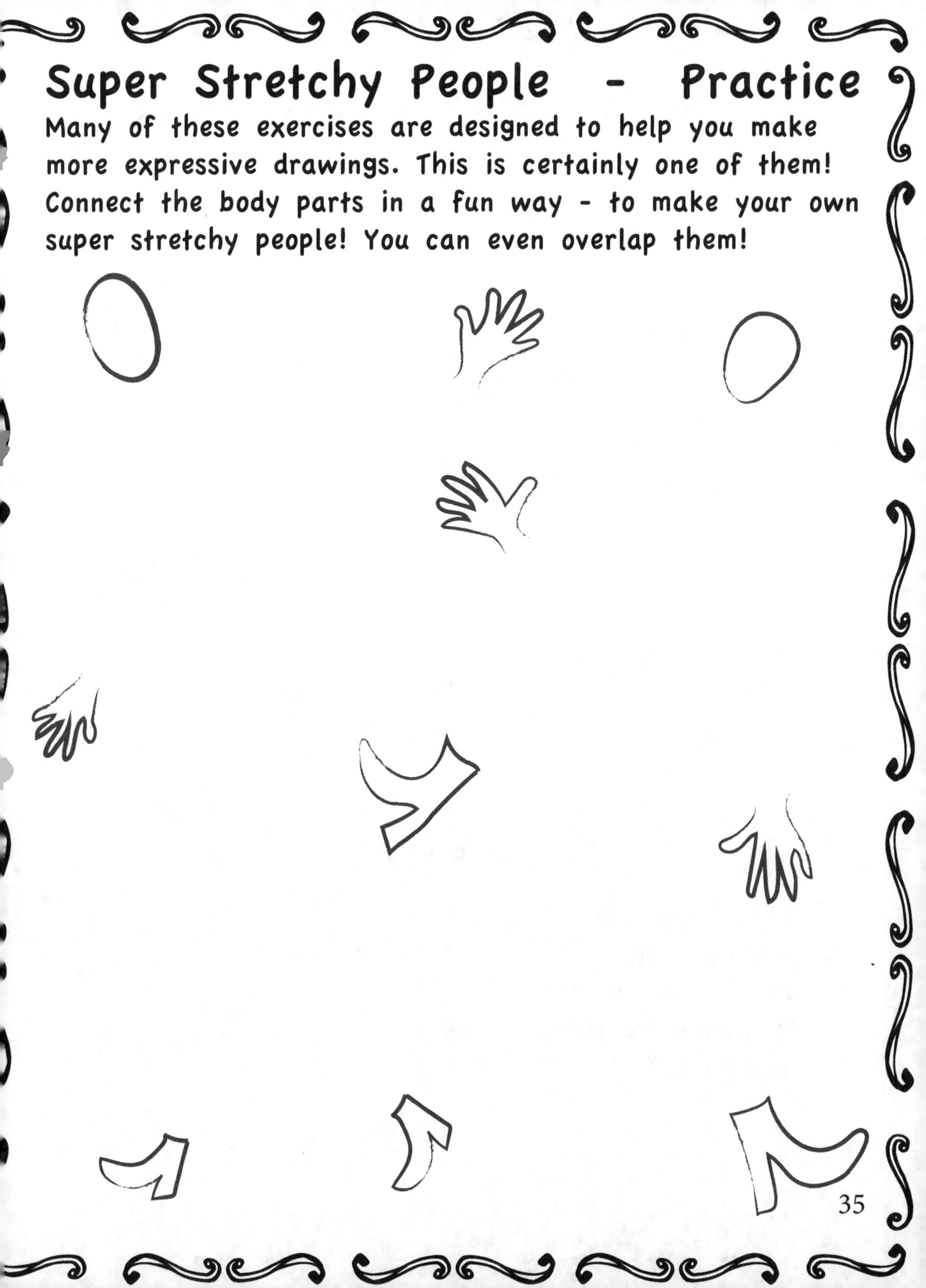

Exercise 15   Bulging eye people

In this exercise we shall emphasize certain features, like eyes. Make them bulge out of the head!

The person can smile or act surprised to support the pop-eyed expression.

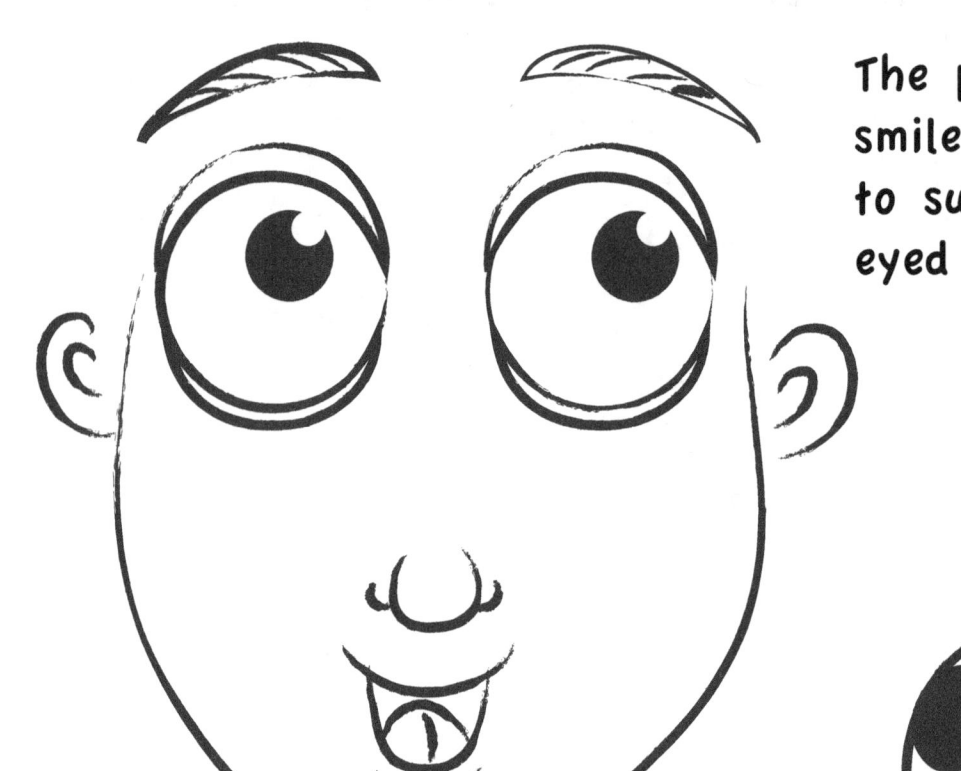

You can add details, like veins to emphasize the bulging effect.

Bulging eye people - Practice

Now draw in some bulging eyes, use details like eyebrows and eyelids to show the effects.

Exercise 16
Playing with body proportions

Here we will play with making some body parts longer than they normally are.

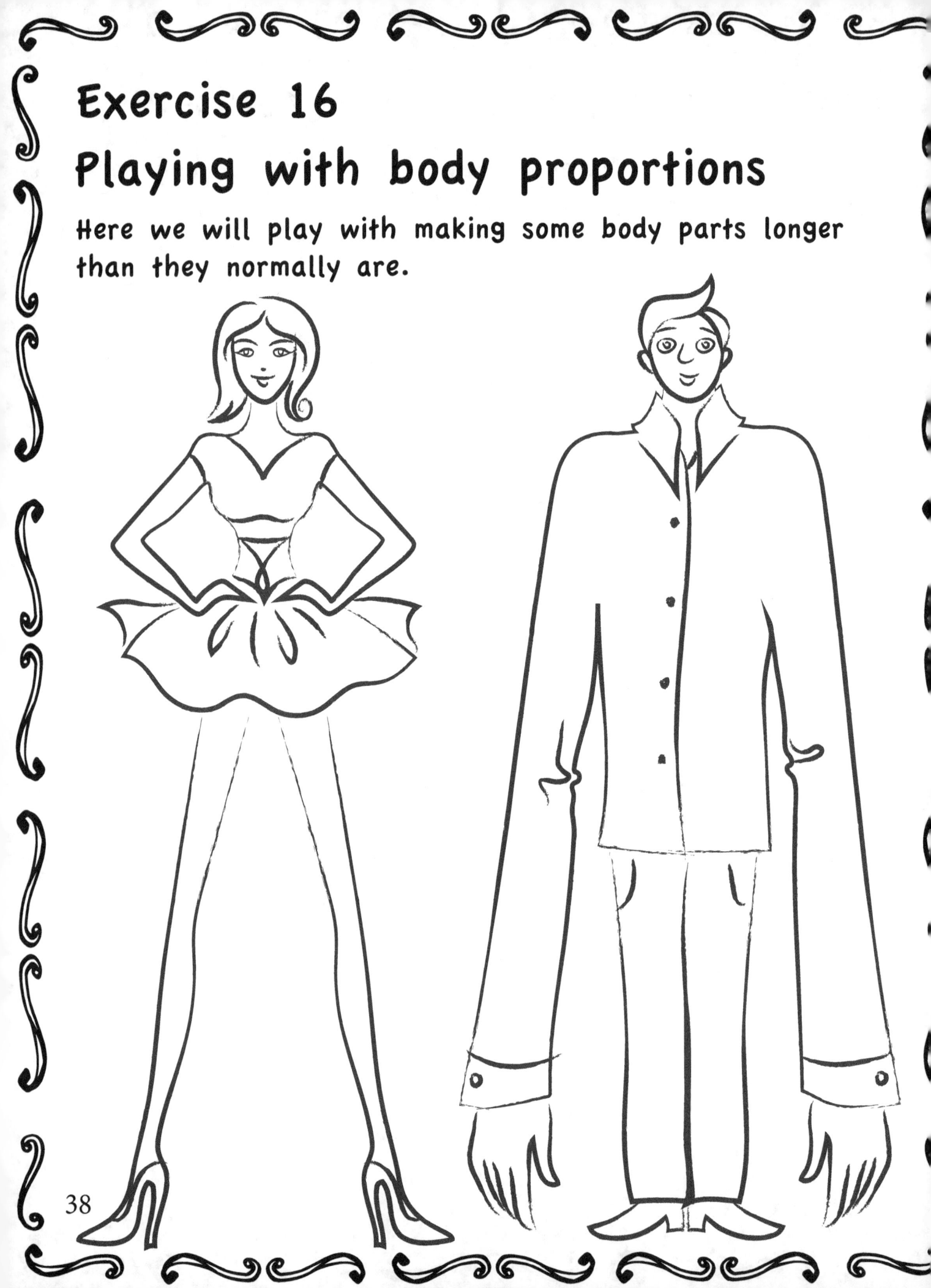

Distorted body proportions - Practice

Now add your own versions of distorted proportions. Make these folks have either long arms, long legs or long necks, etc.

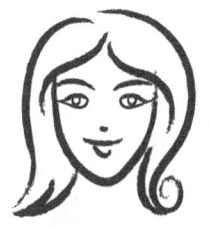 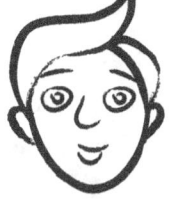

Exercise 17   Room in a sphere

Here we will create a room within a sphere. We can put a person, sitting in the foreground. The perspective is extreme and a bit warped and rounded.

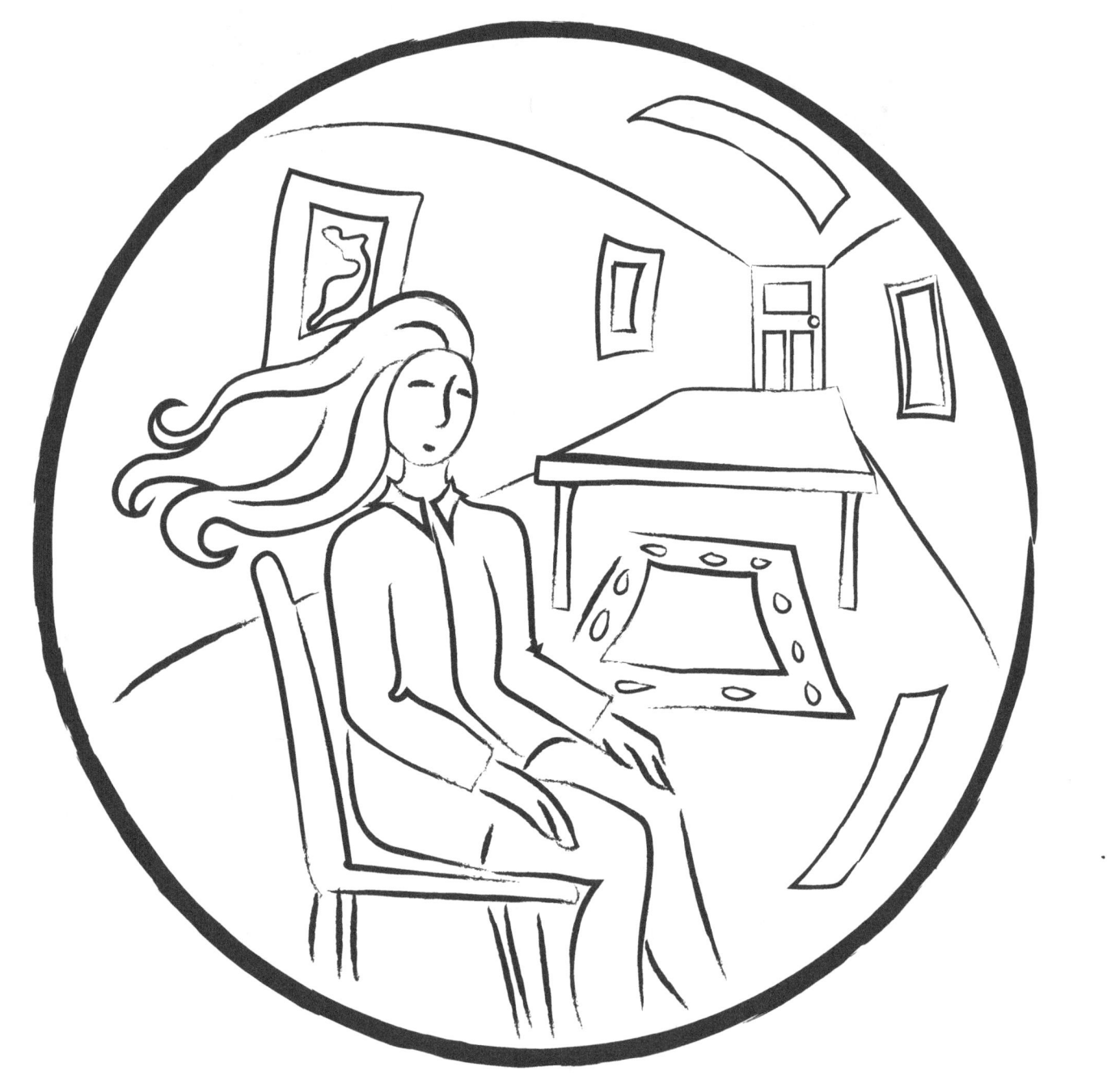

Room in a sphere - Practice

Draw in your own objects within the room and a person sitting on a chair. You can add shine shapes on the side to make an illusion of a ball.

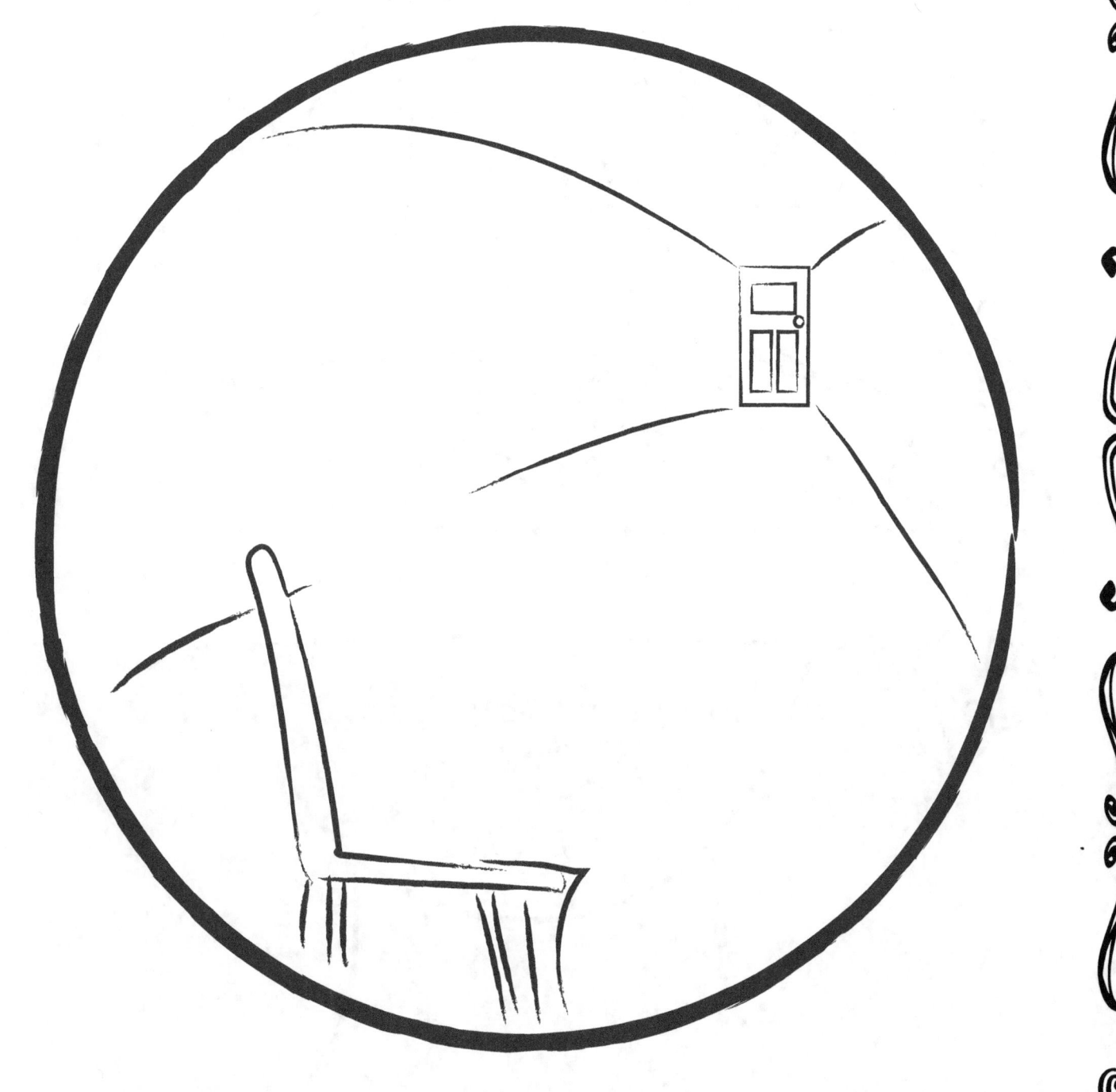

Exercise 18   Face-Object

In this exercise let us combine a human face with an object, such as an old fashioned phone.

Face-Object - Practice

Now add an object of your choice to the face. It can be anything, like ordinary objects you find around the house.

Exercise 19 Warped Street

Let us make a drawing of a warped street. What would it look like if all of the houses were sort of "dancing" along the street?

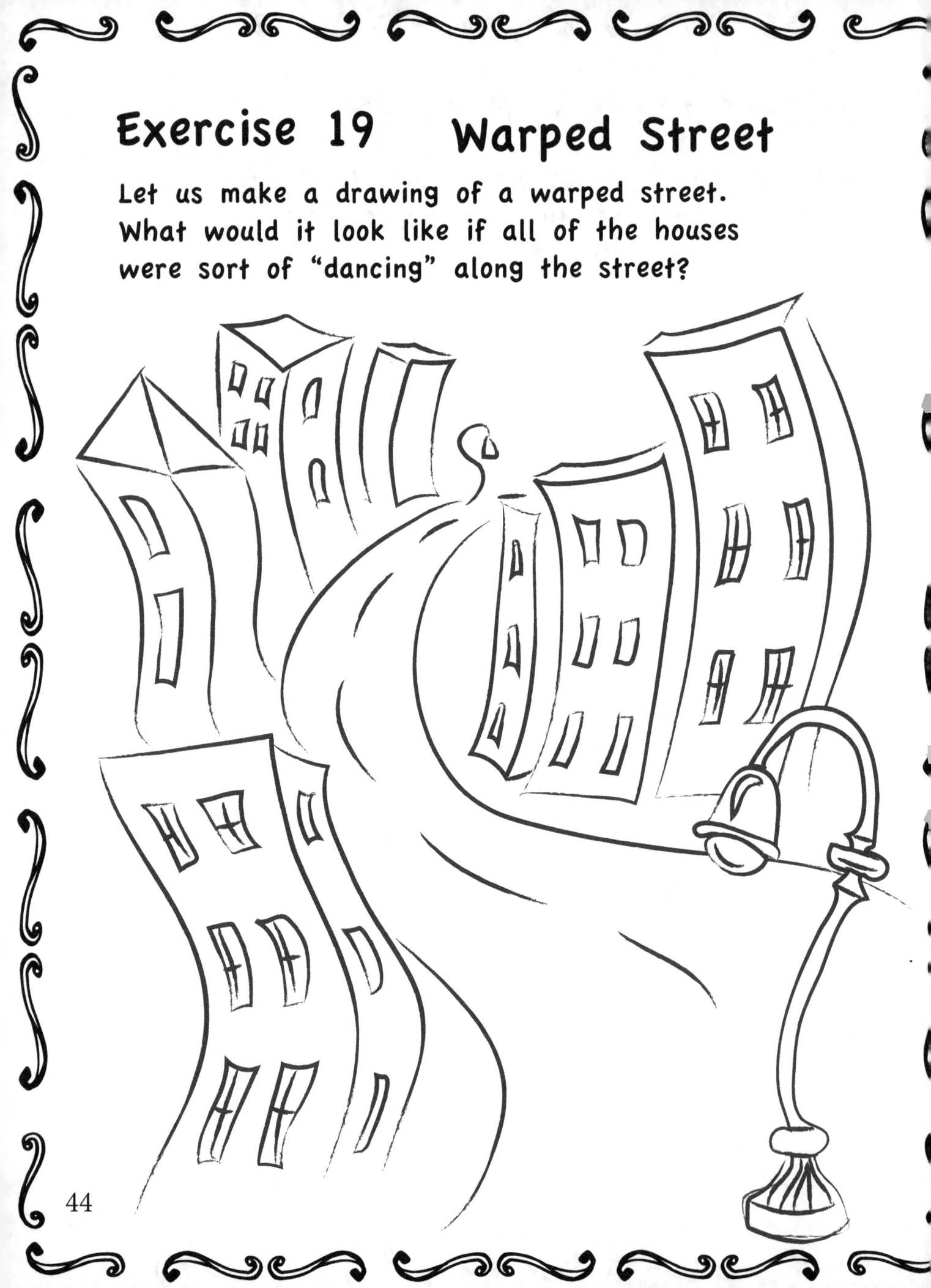

Warped Street   -   Practice

Now let us practice drawing a warped dancing town. As buildings get farther away, they get smaller. Buildings that are closer, overlap those that are behind them. Make buildings curve as if they are dancing.

45

Exercise 20   Weird locations

In this exercise we will place people and landscapes in unusual locations. It makes for a really interesting picture and juxtaposition.

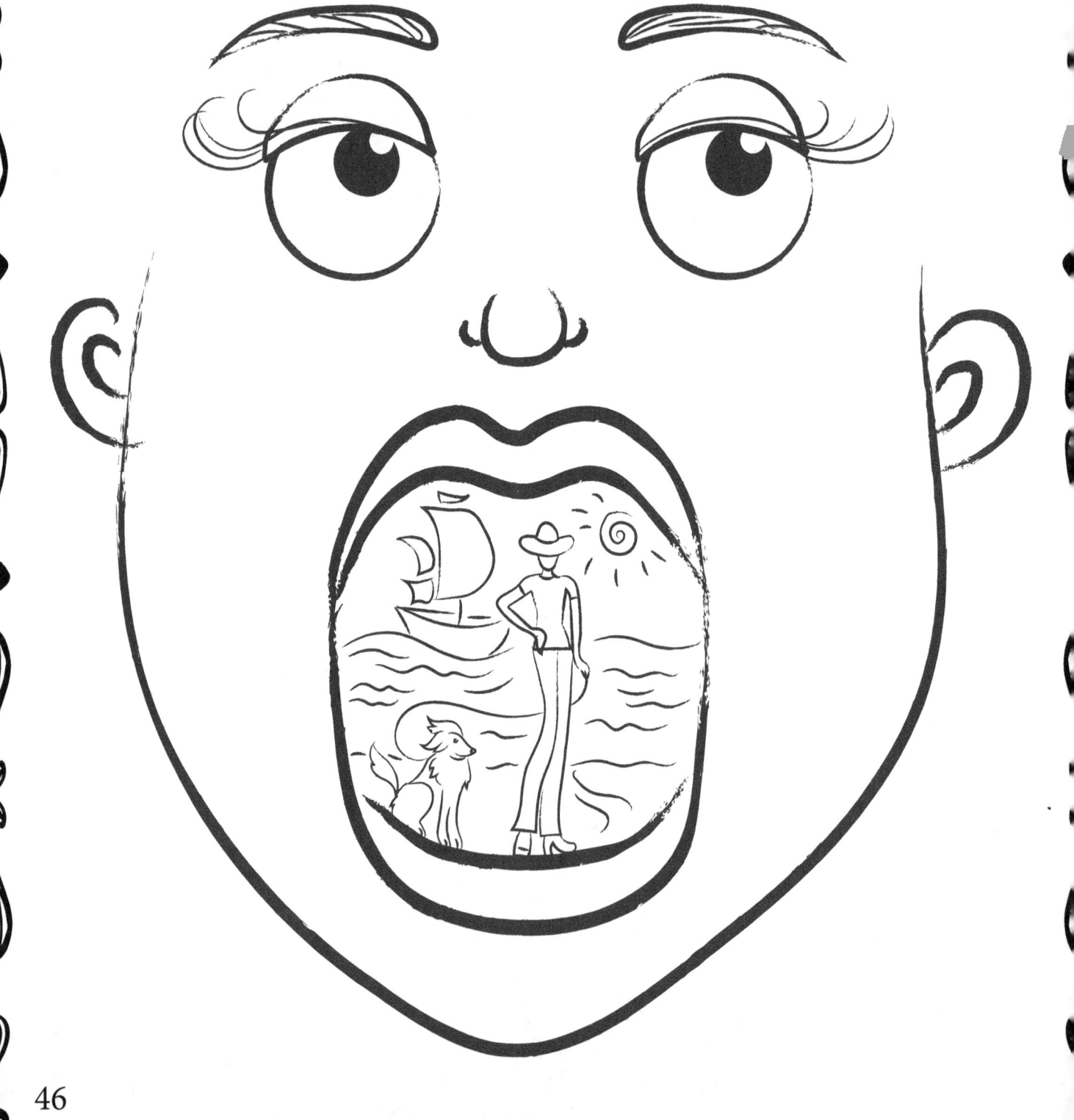

Weird locations - Practice

Now draw your own picture inside the mouth. Make it something fun and playful. We are not after a horror theme, but something interesting and intriguing.

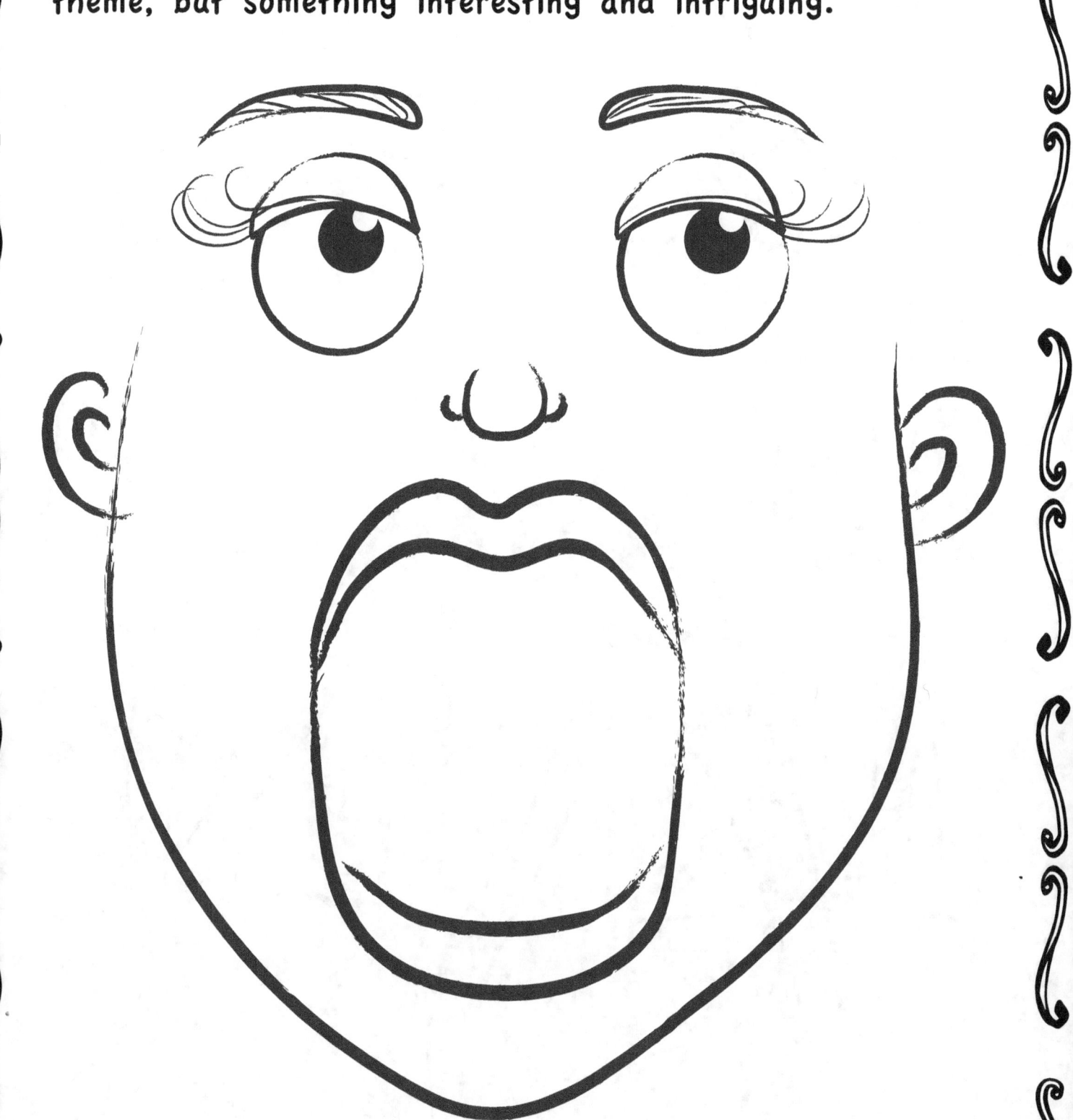

Exercise 21   Fantastical animals

Let us combine an elephant and a zebra. We can jot down a silhouette of a town in the background.

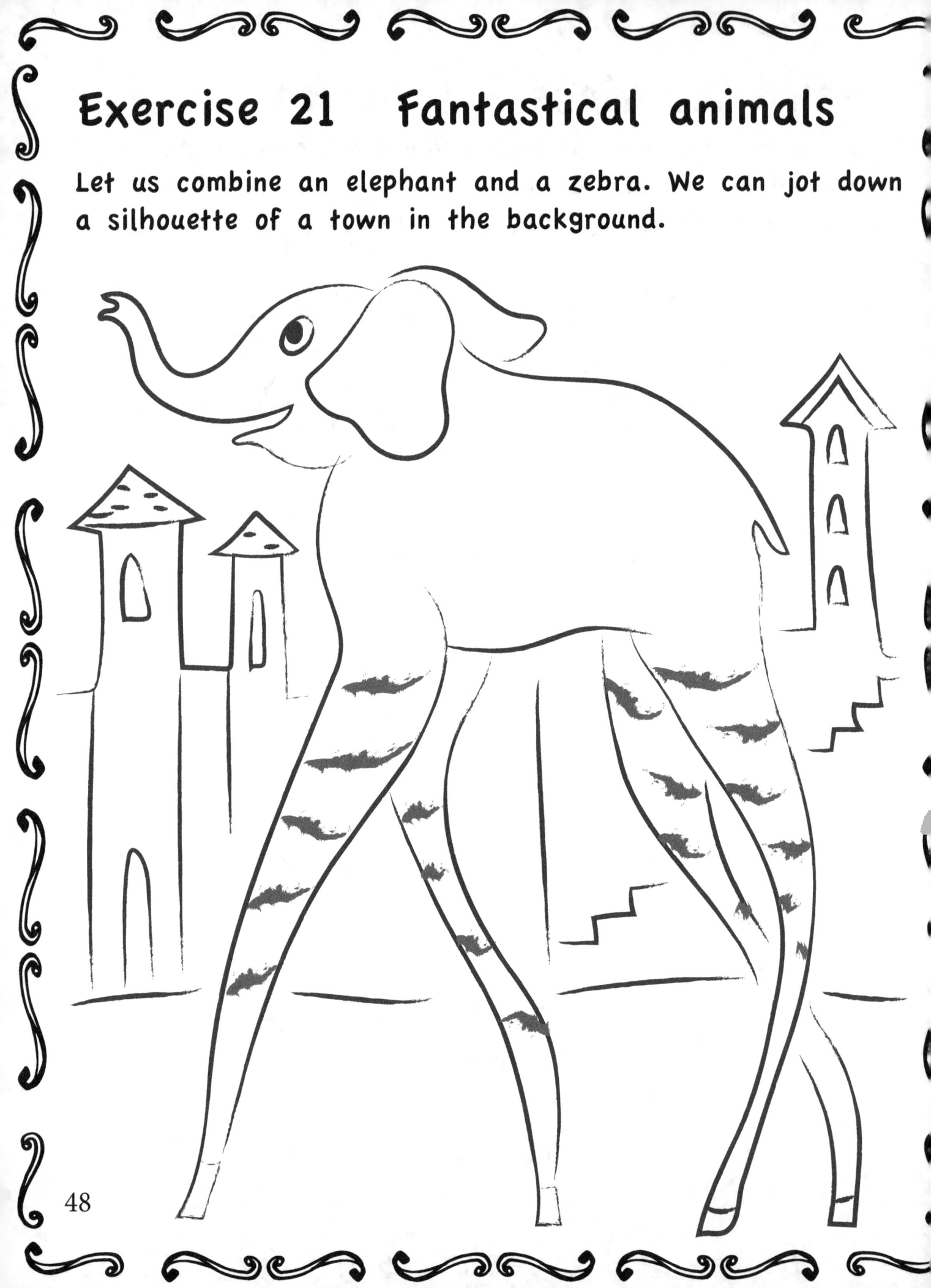

Fantastical animals - Practice

Now create your own fantastical elephant or giraffe, or any other animal. Fill in the details of the town too.

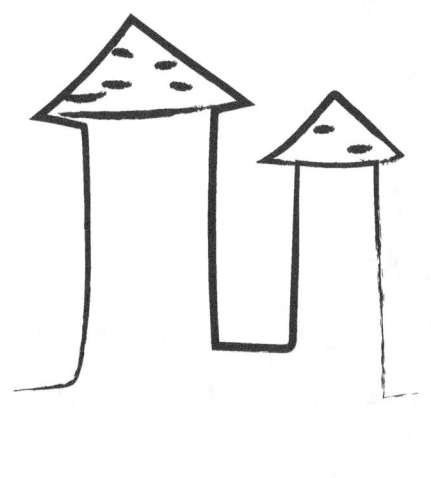
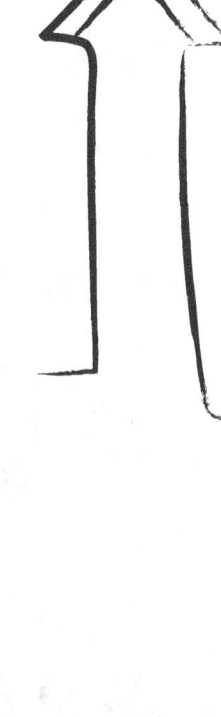

Exercise 22   Flower hair

Here let us make flower vine hair. You can play with different lengths and flowers.

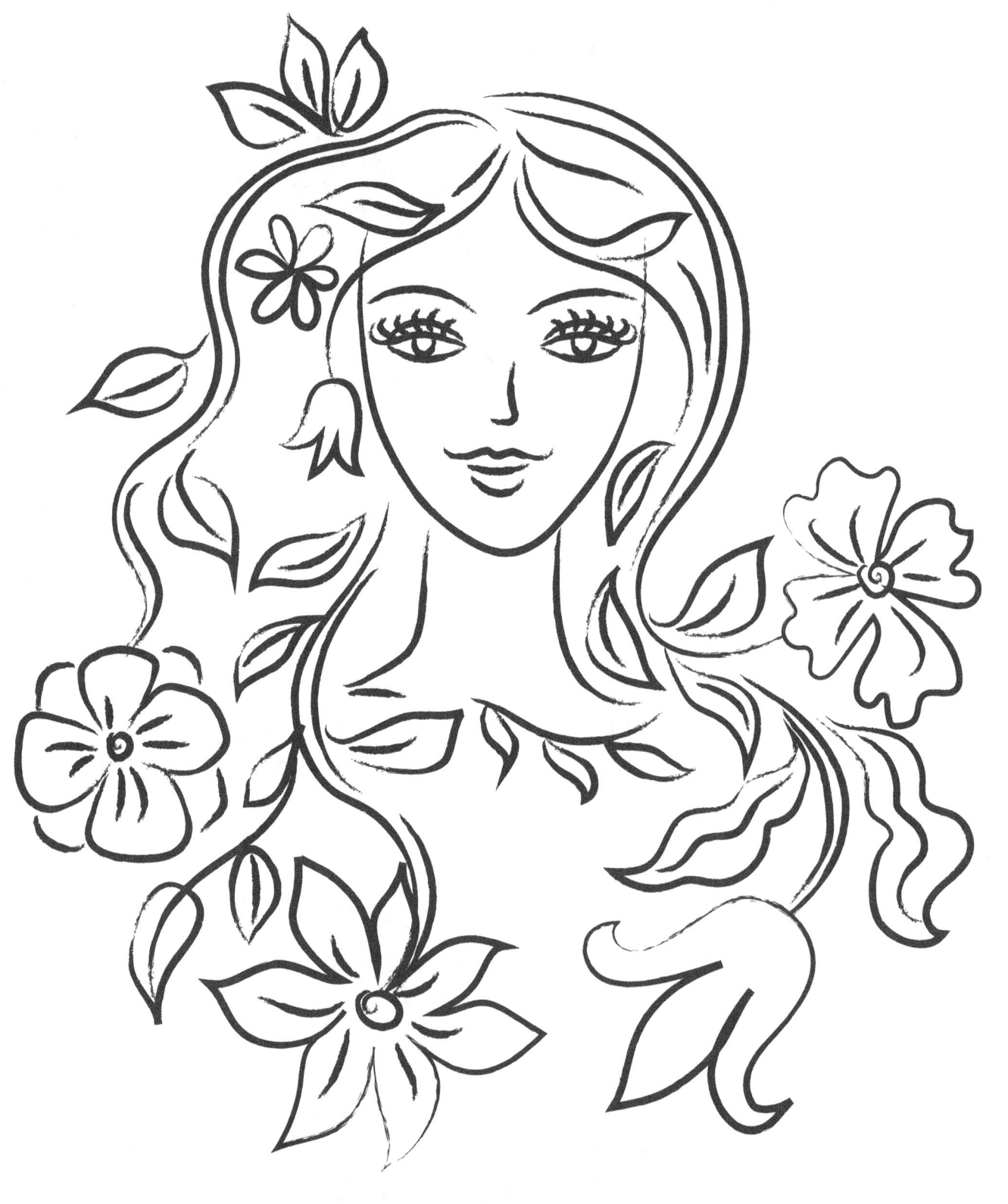

Flower hair - Practice

Now add your own flower hair. Add exotic flowers and leaves. Make them weave in and out in creative ways.

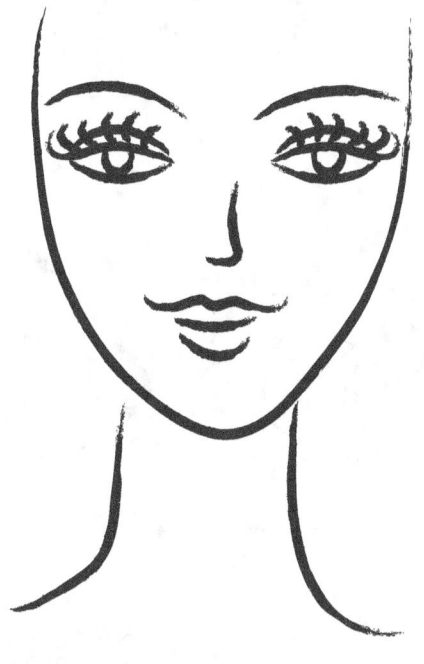

Exercise 23 Cat and Human hybrid

In this exercise, we will combine a human and cat face in one. You can also do a dog/human combo.

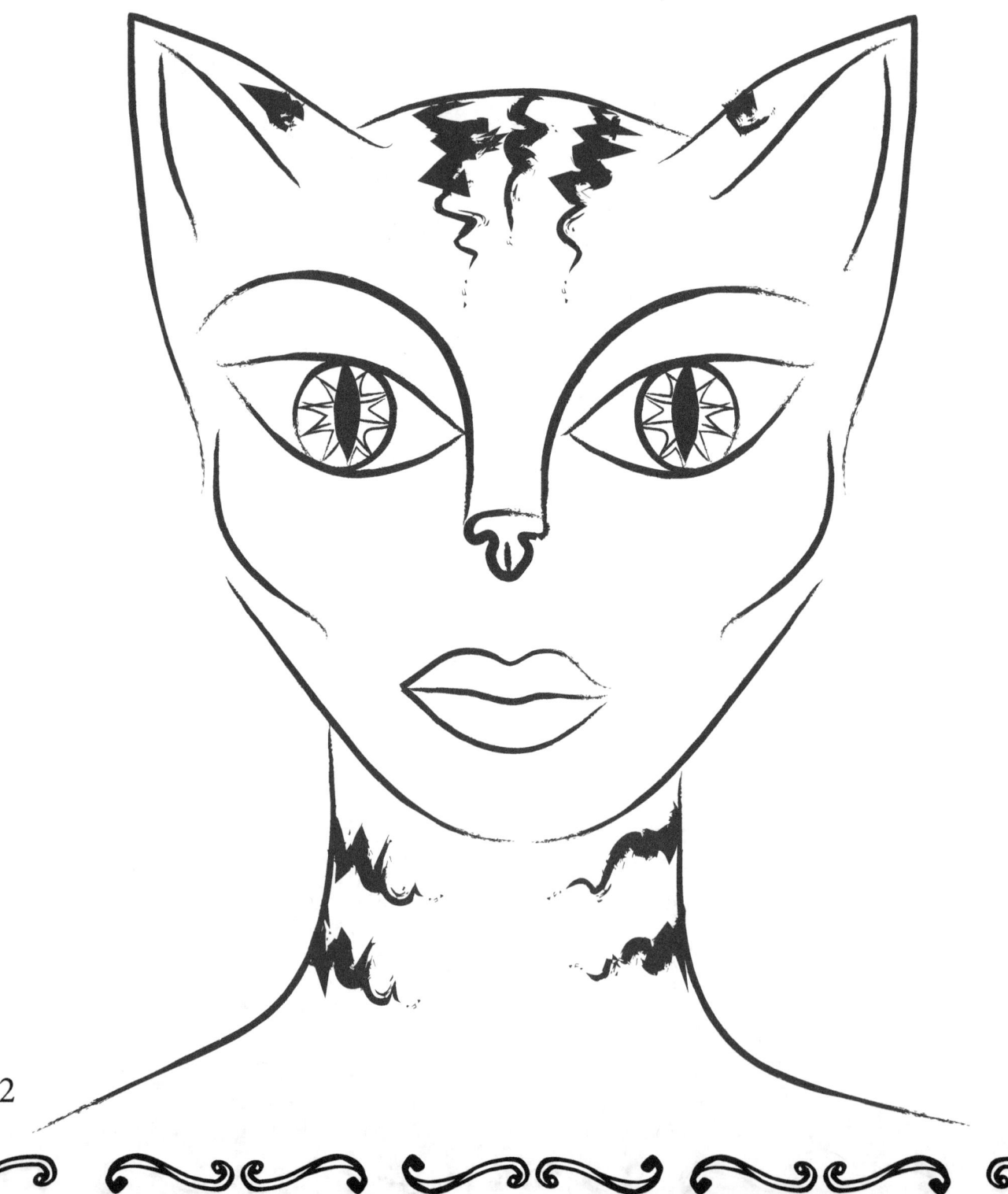

Cat and Human hybrid - Practice

Now practice combining your favorite pet and human faces in one.

53

Exercise 24
Living room outdoors

In this exercise we will put living room objects in a forest or an outdoor scene.

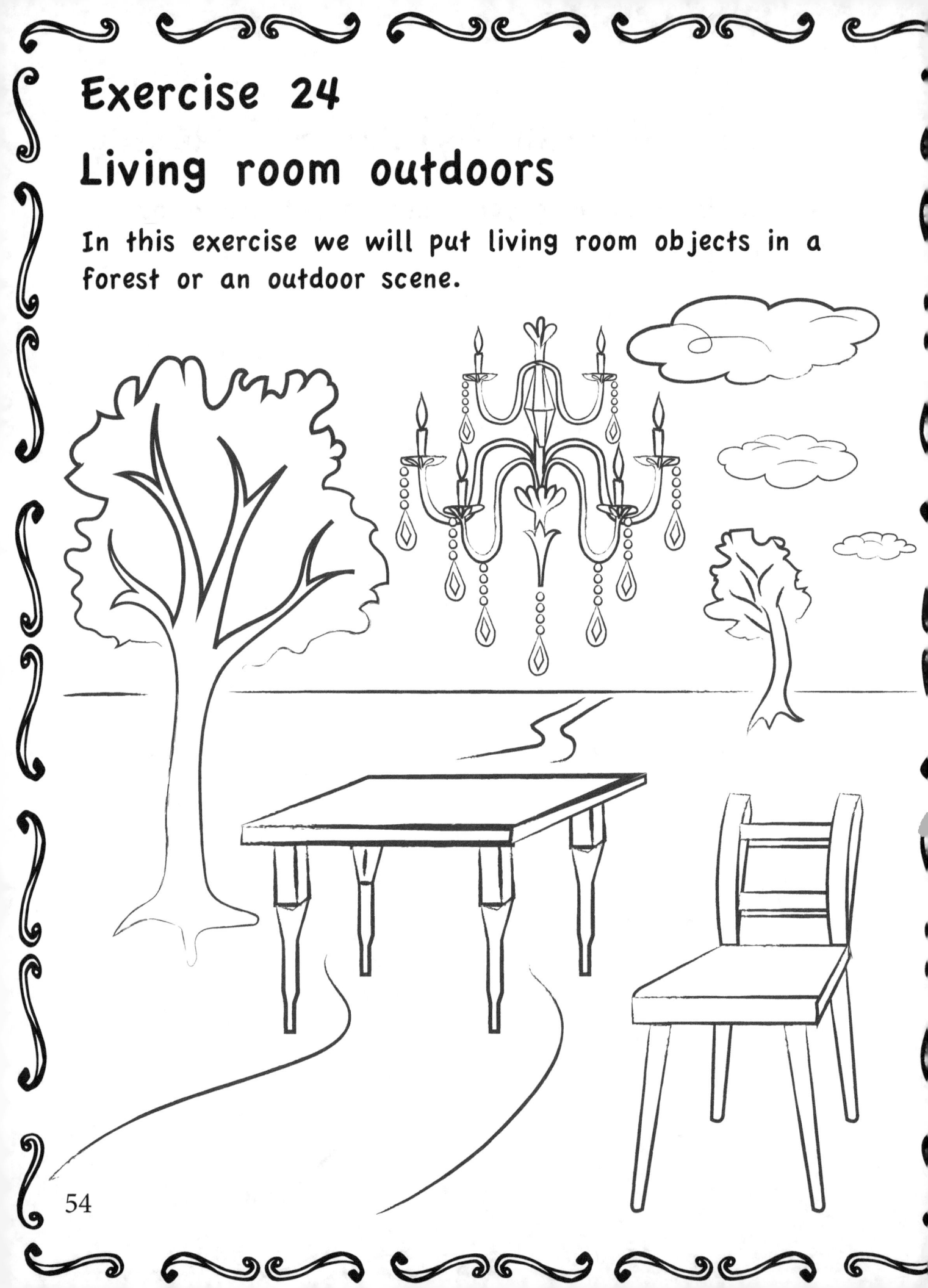

Living room outdoors - Practice

Now you can make your own outdoor living room. You can add any objects you find in your own house, like chair, couch, table, lamps, etc.

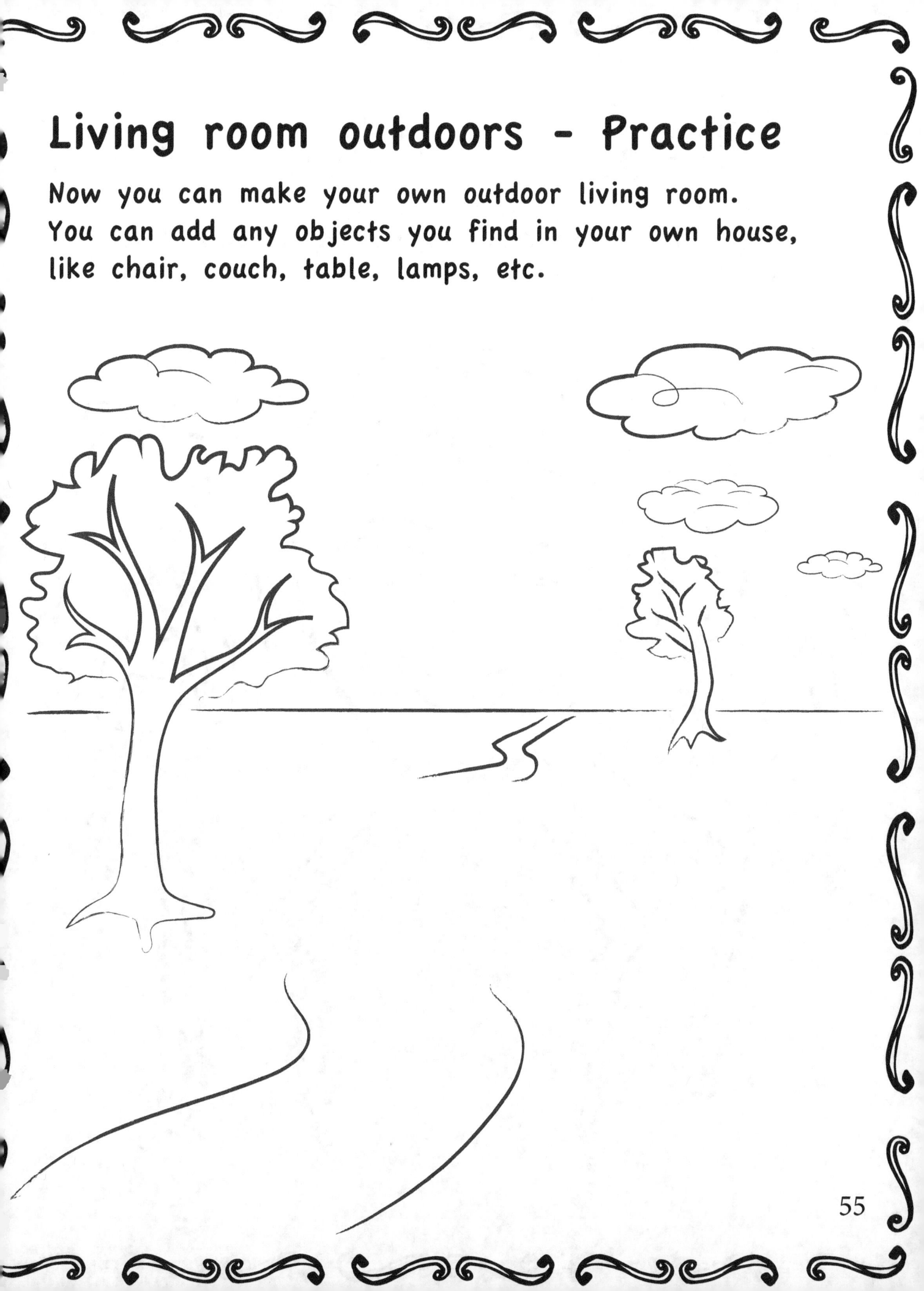

Exercise 25   Creepy Spider

Here we will combine a human head and spider legs. Now we have a creepy creature.

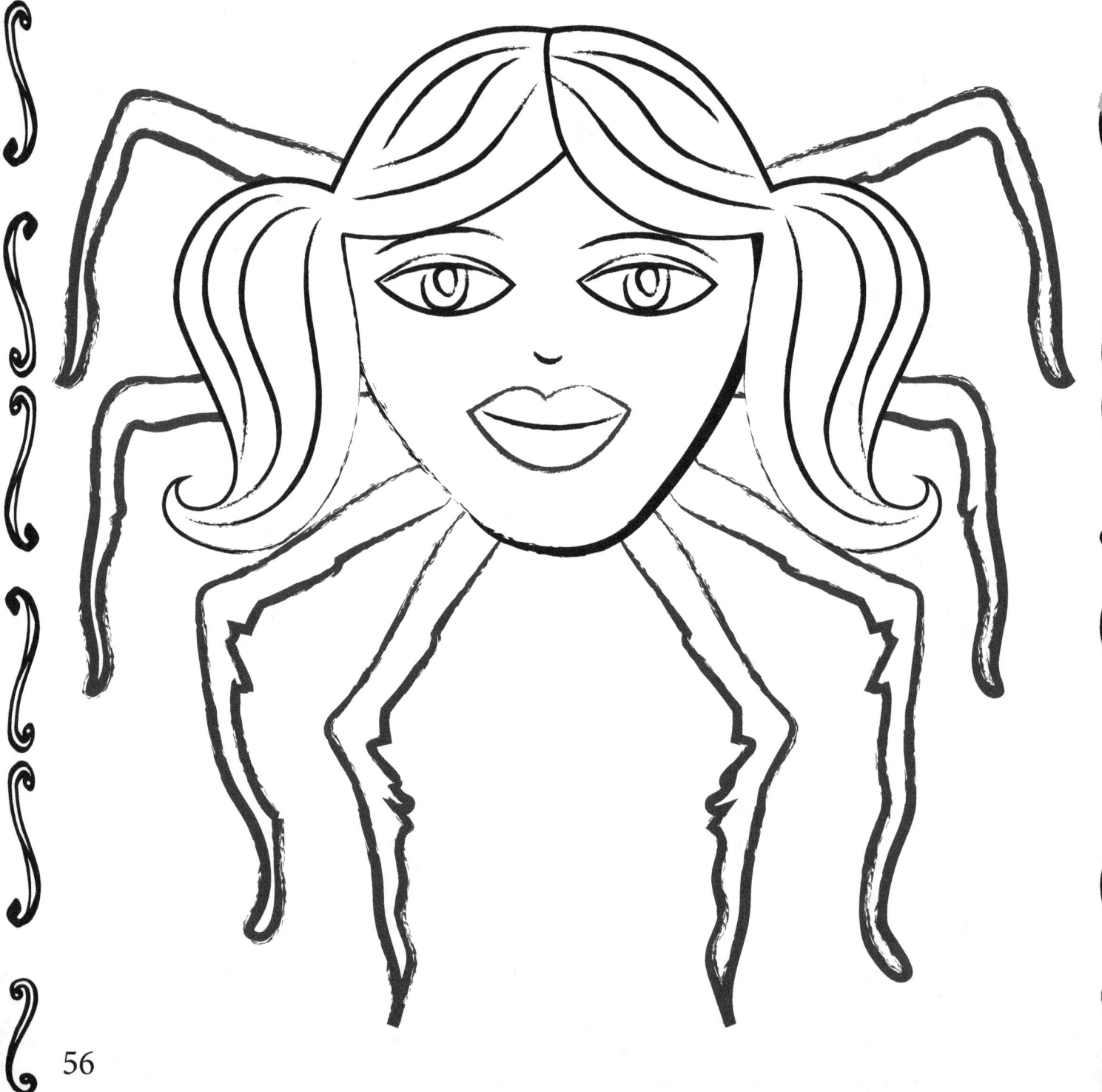

Creepy Spider - Practice

Now you can do the same thing. Add a head to this spider. It can be any head, human, animal, or a spider of your imagination.

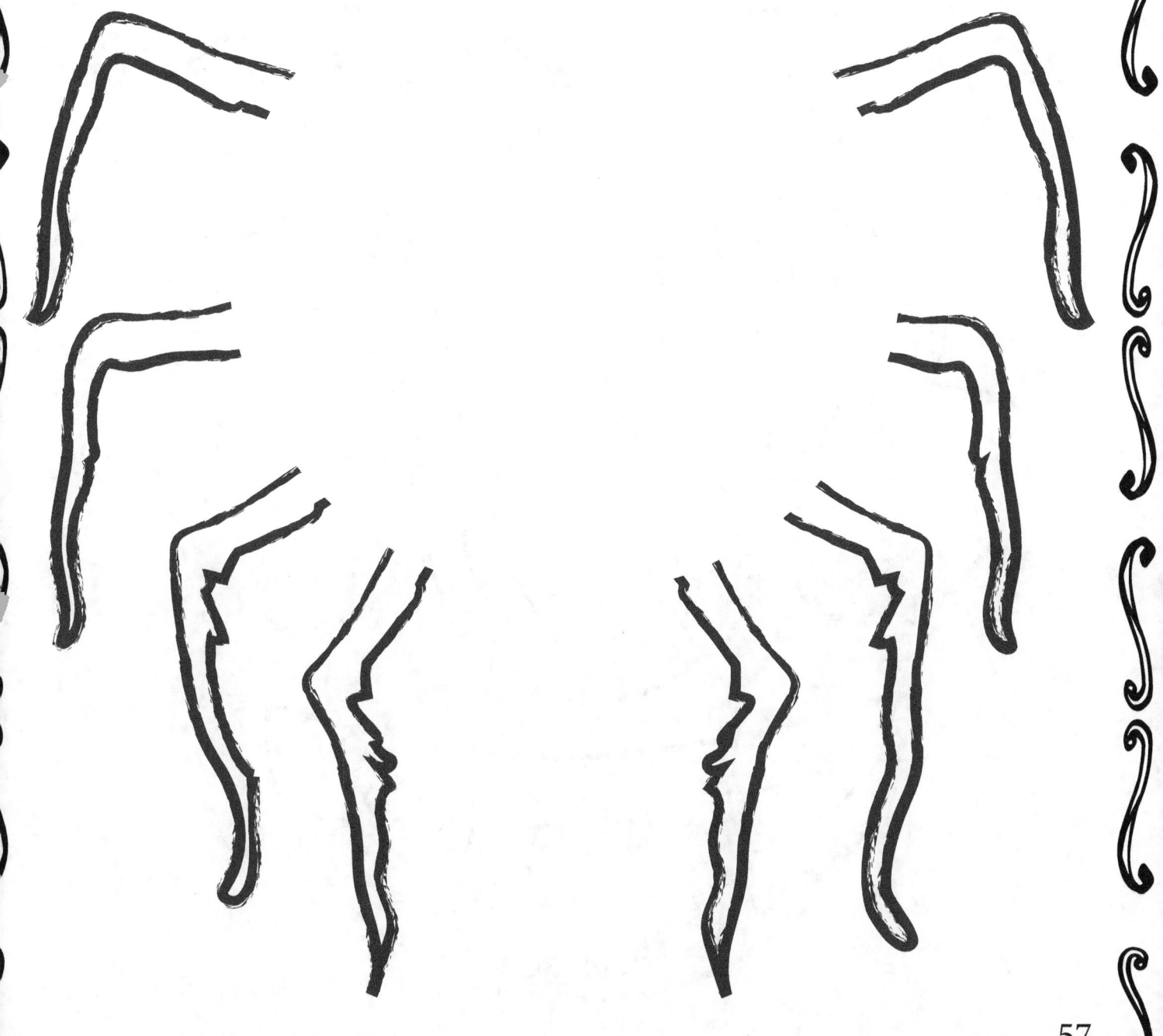

Exercise 26
Face made of fruit and veggies

Here we will make a face out of fruit and veggies!

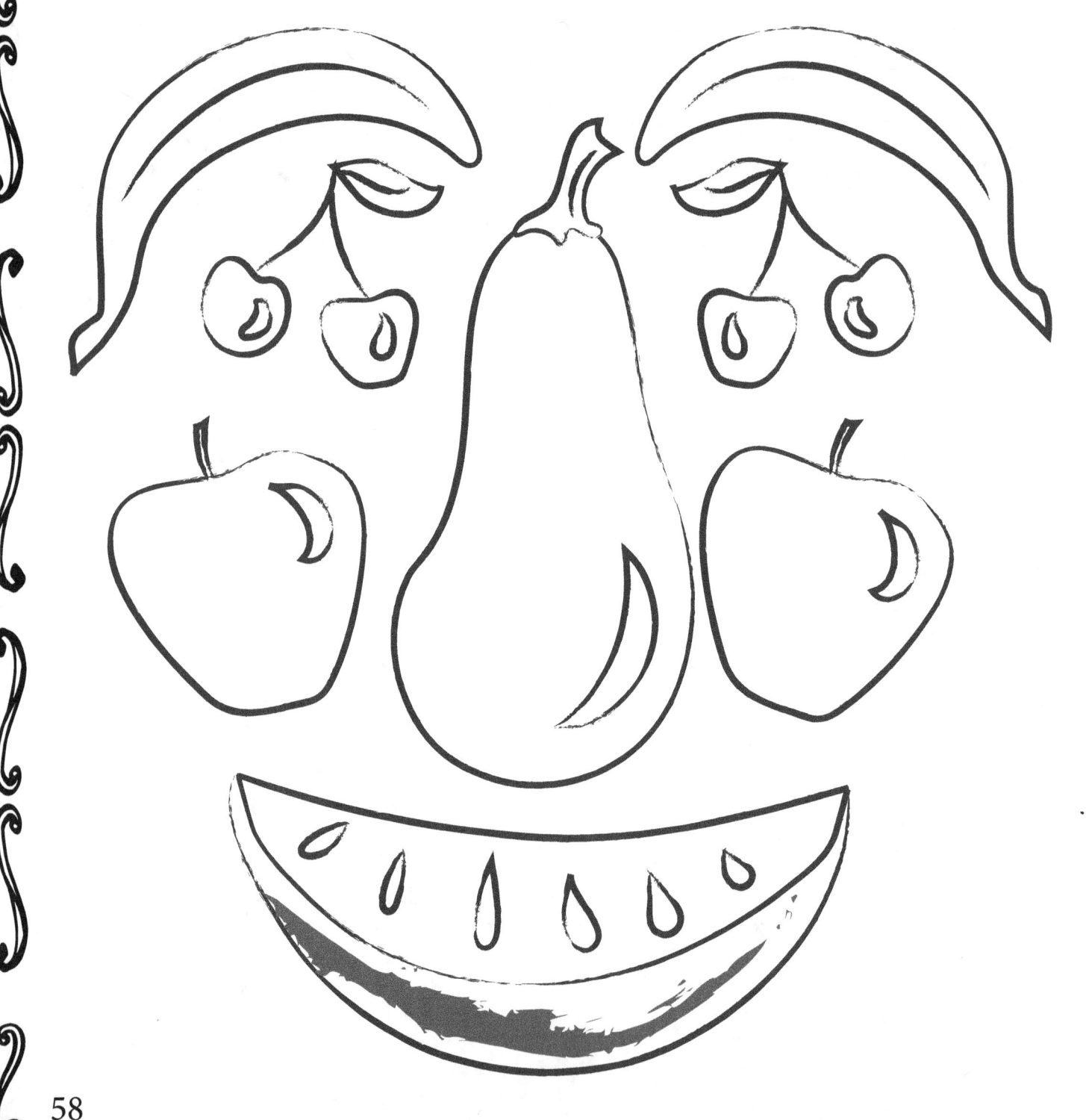

Face made of fruit and veggies Practice

Now create your own face out of these fruit and veggies.

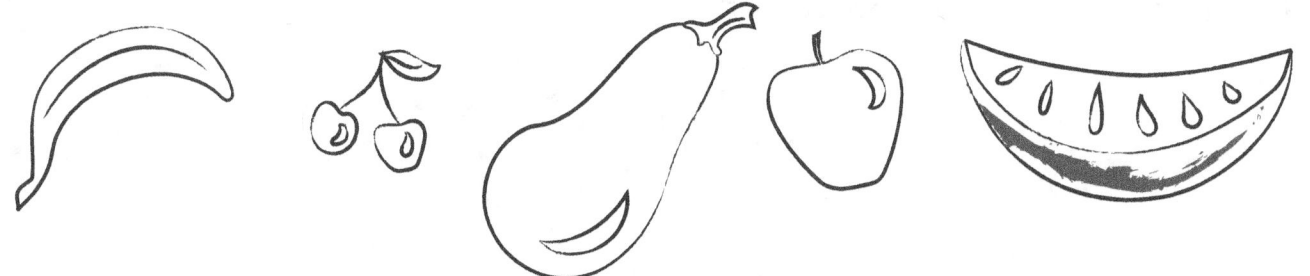

Exercise 27
A shoe that's also a house

In this exercise we will make a house out of a shoe. We can add a background.

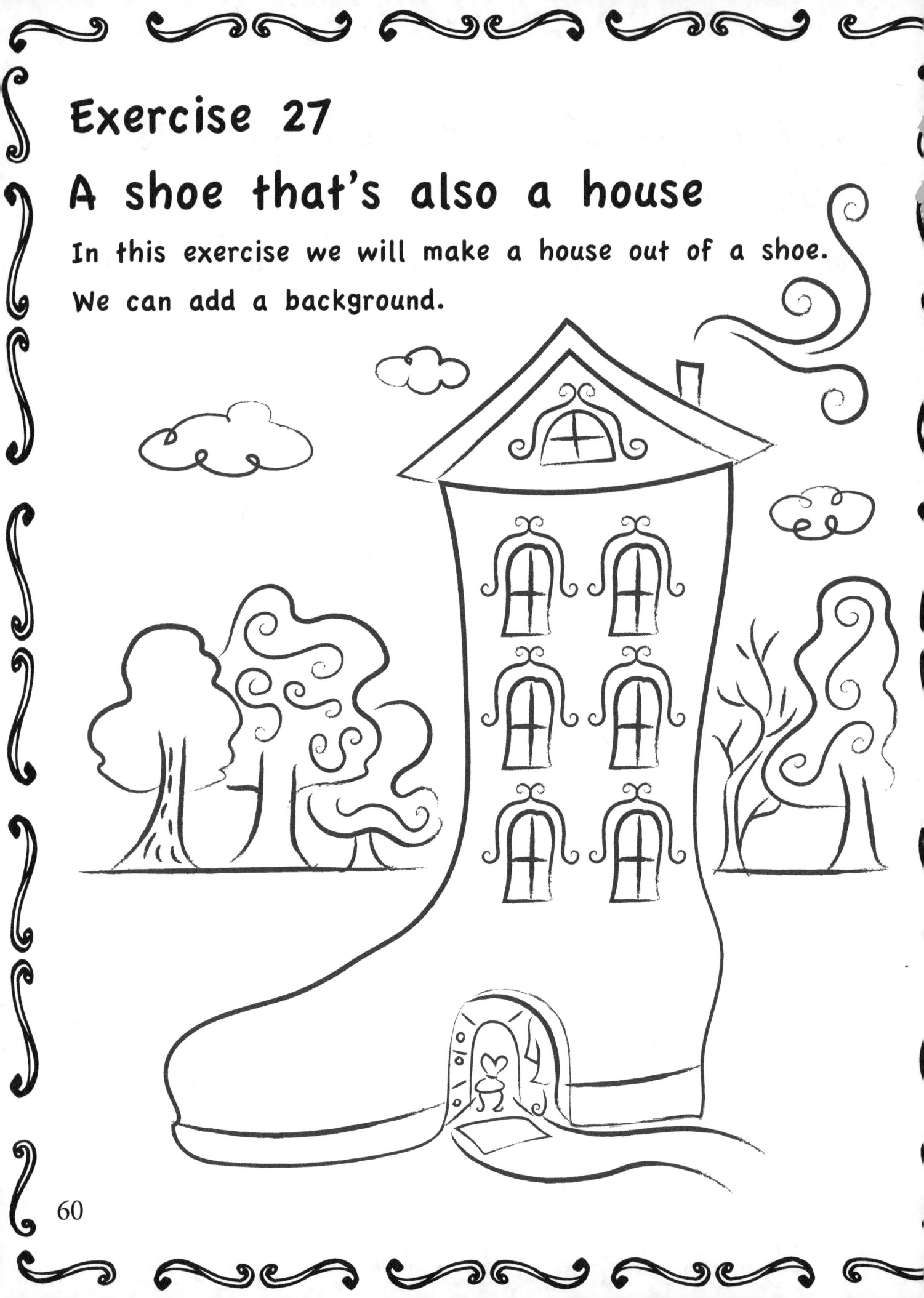

Shoe House - Practice

Now add your own shoe house to the background.

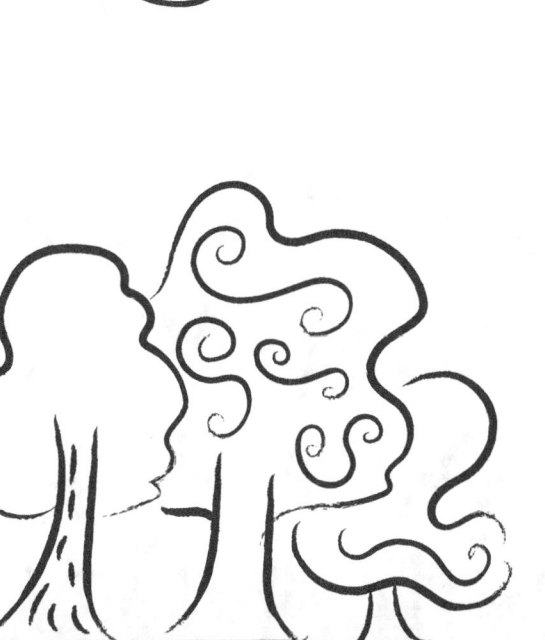
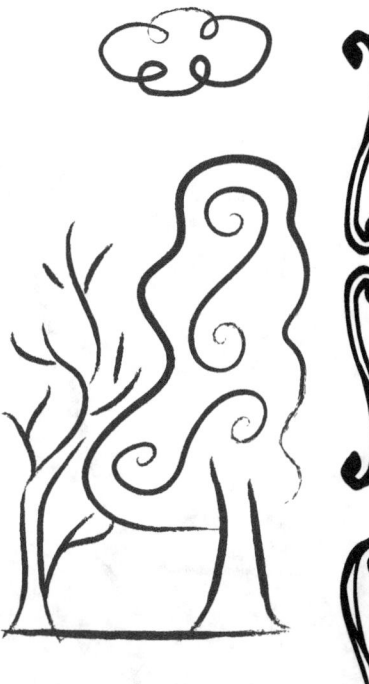

Exercise 28 — Man with a hole

Now let us draw a man with a hole in his body, through which we can see the background.

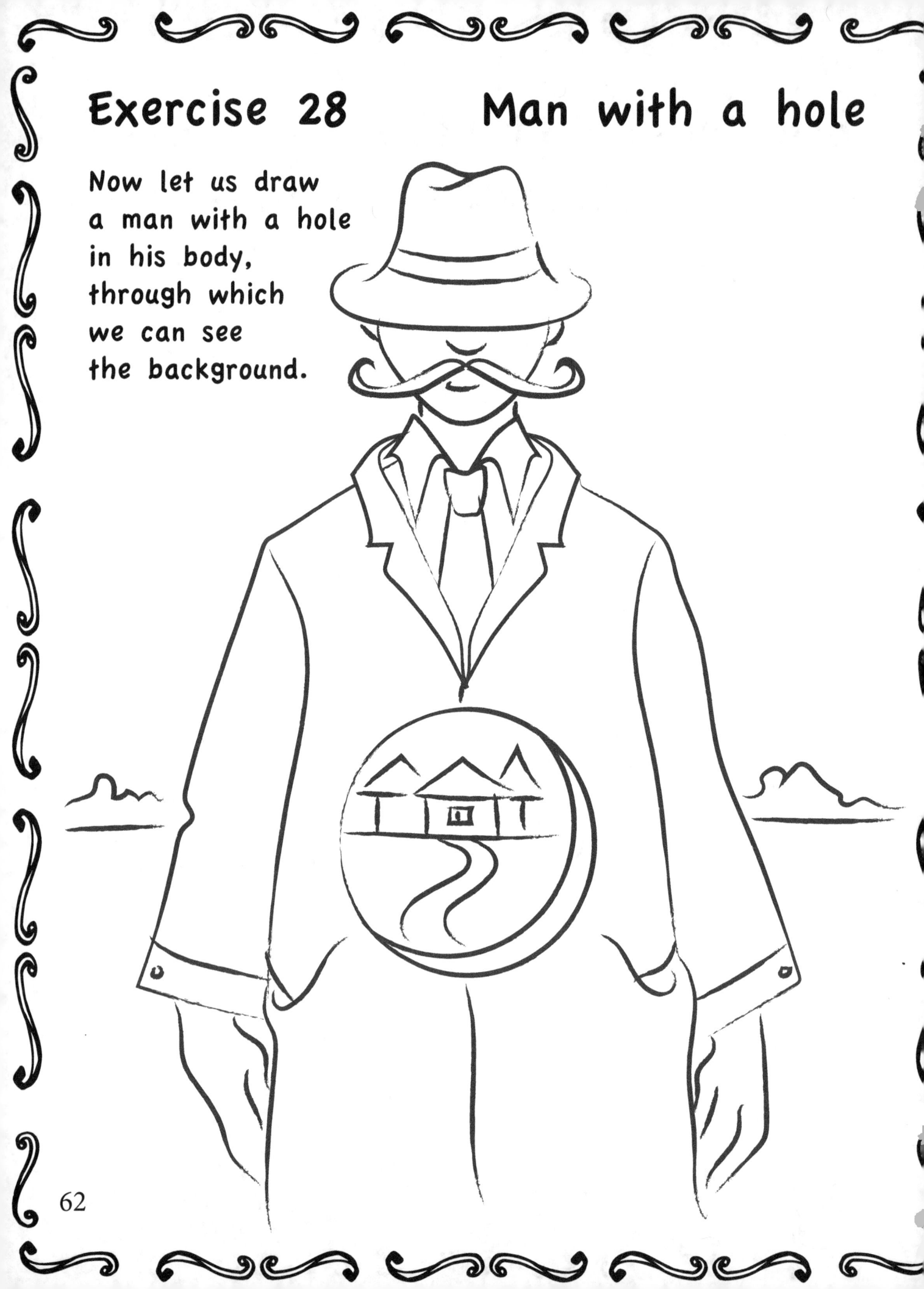

62

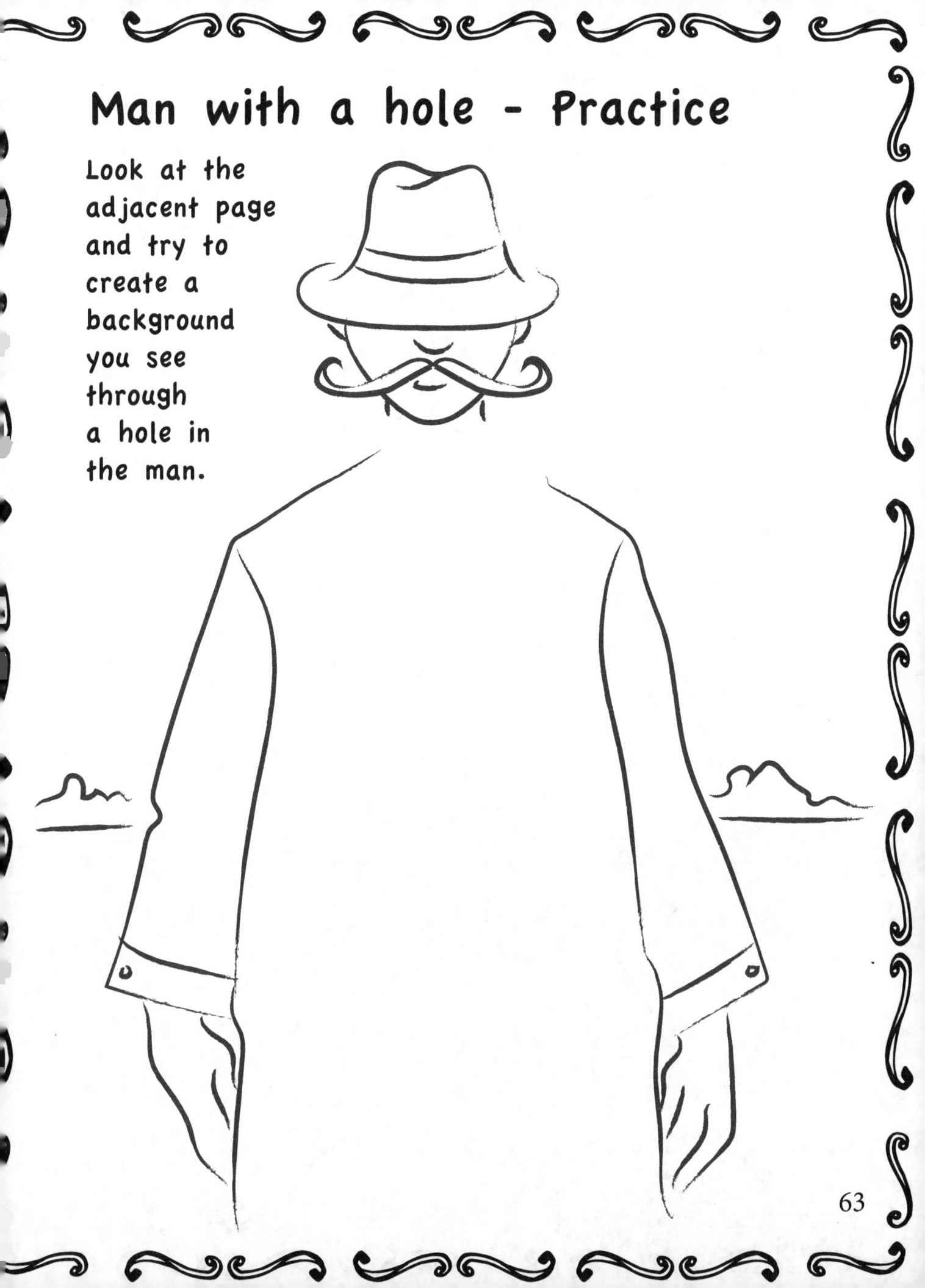

Exercise 29   Jumbled body

Let's call this exercise "Unsuccessful teleportation". What if someone got teleported to another place, but came there with their body all jumbled incorrectly?

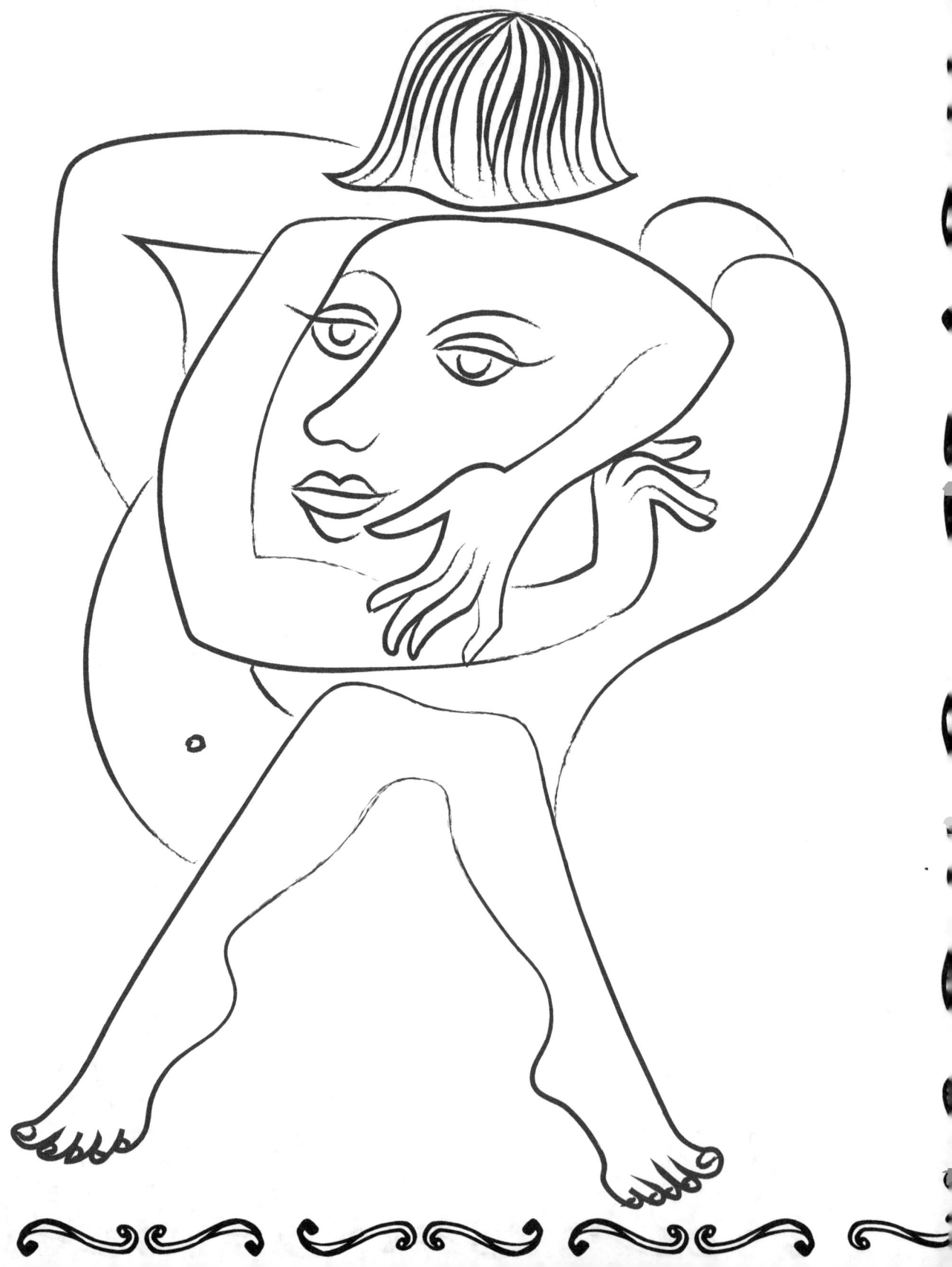

Jumbled body - Practice

Now make your own version of the jumbled body. Use parts like these:

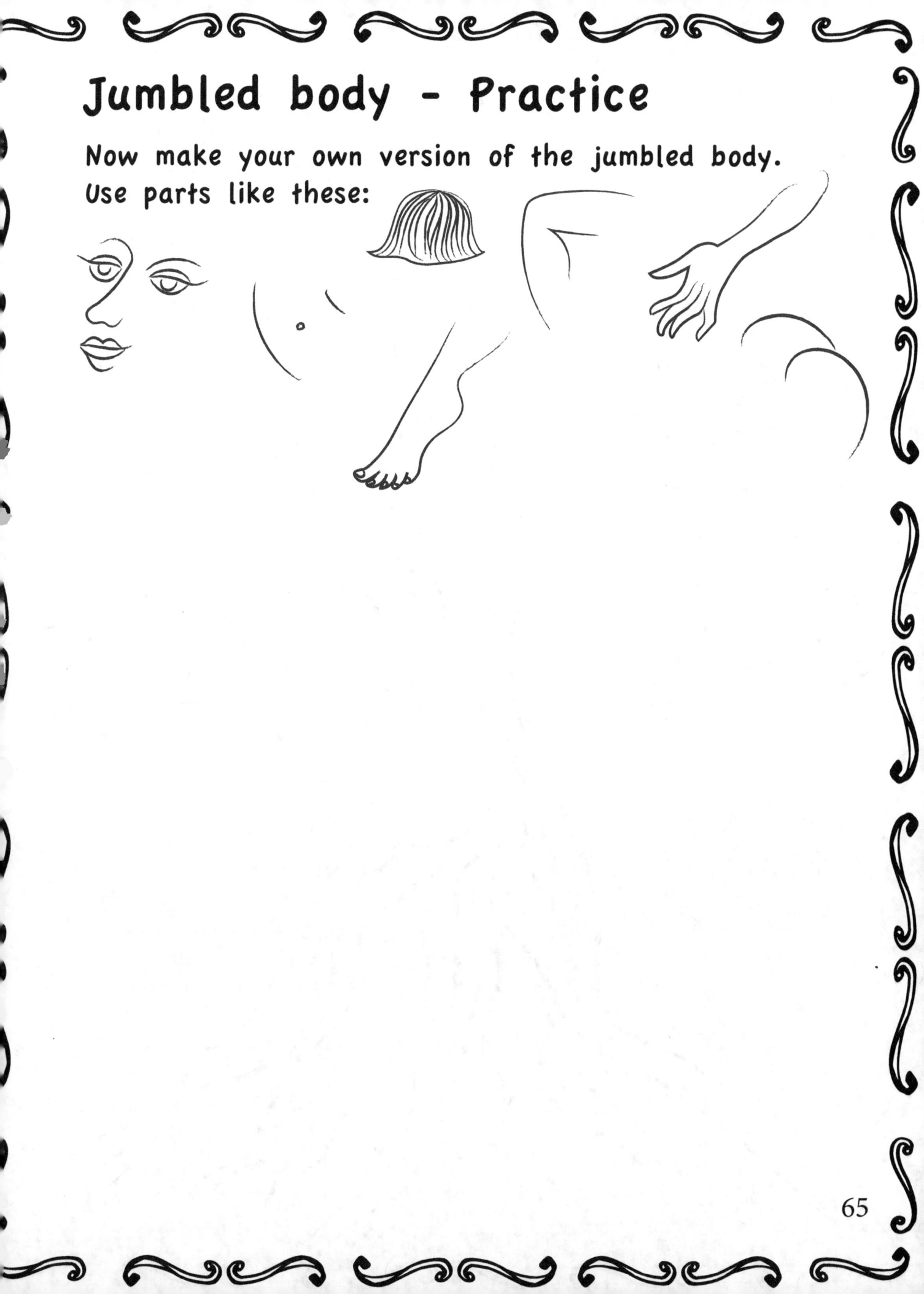

Exercise 30   Tree Person

Imagine if people transformed into trees. How would that look?

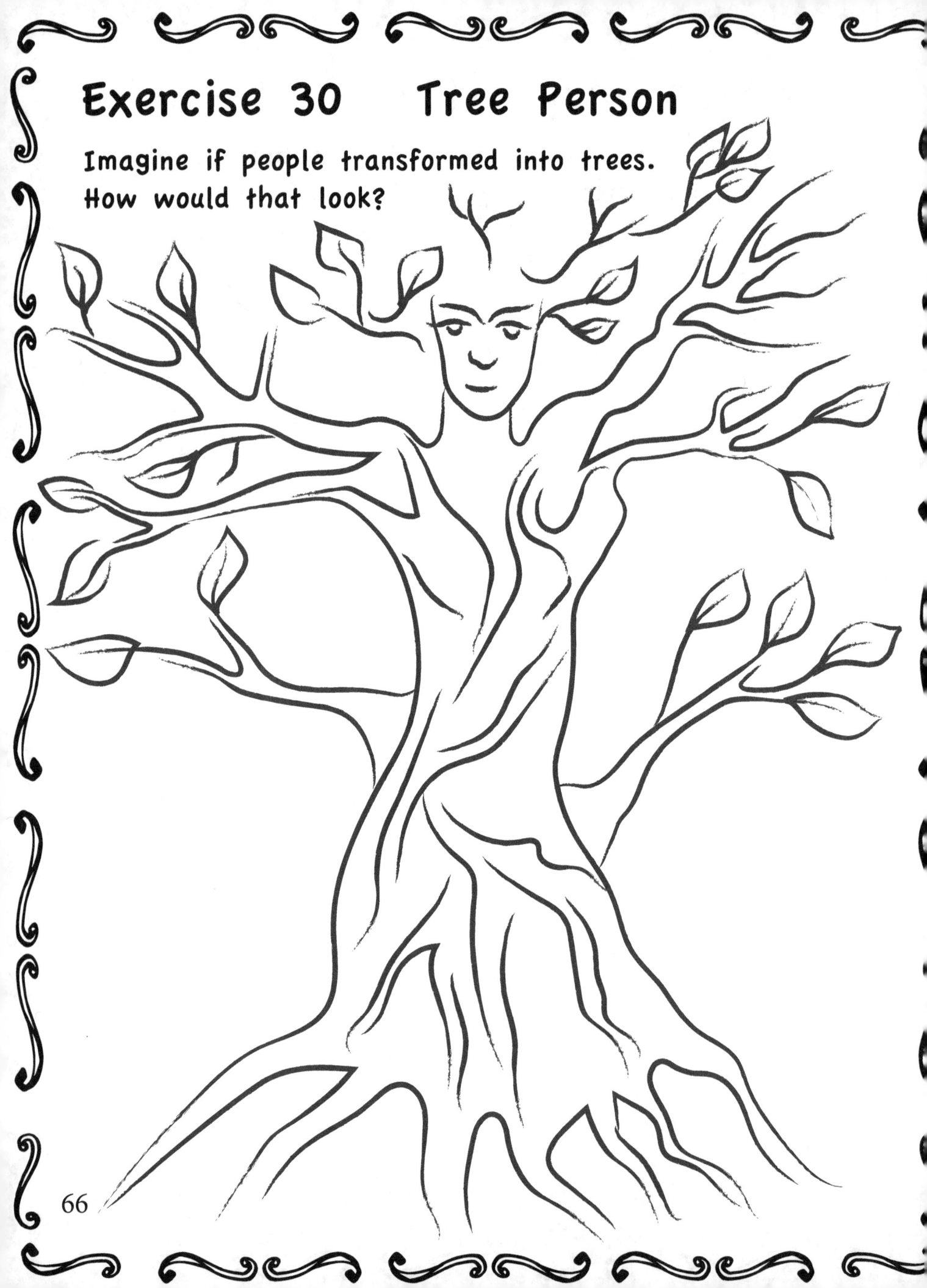

Tree Person - Practice

Now practice adding branches, leaves and roots to your own tree person. You can also add a face.

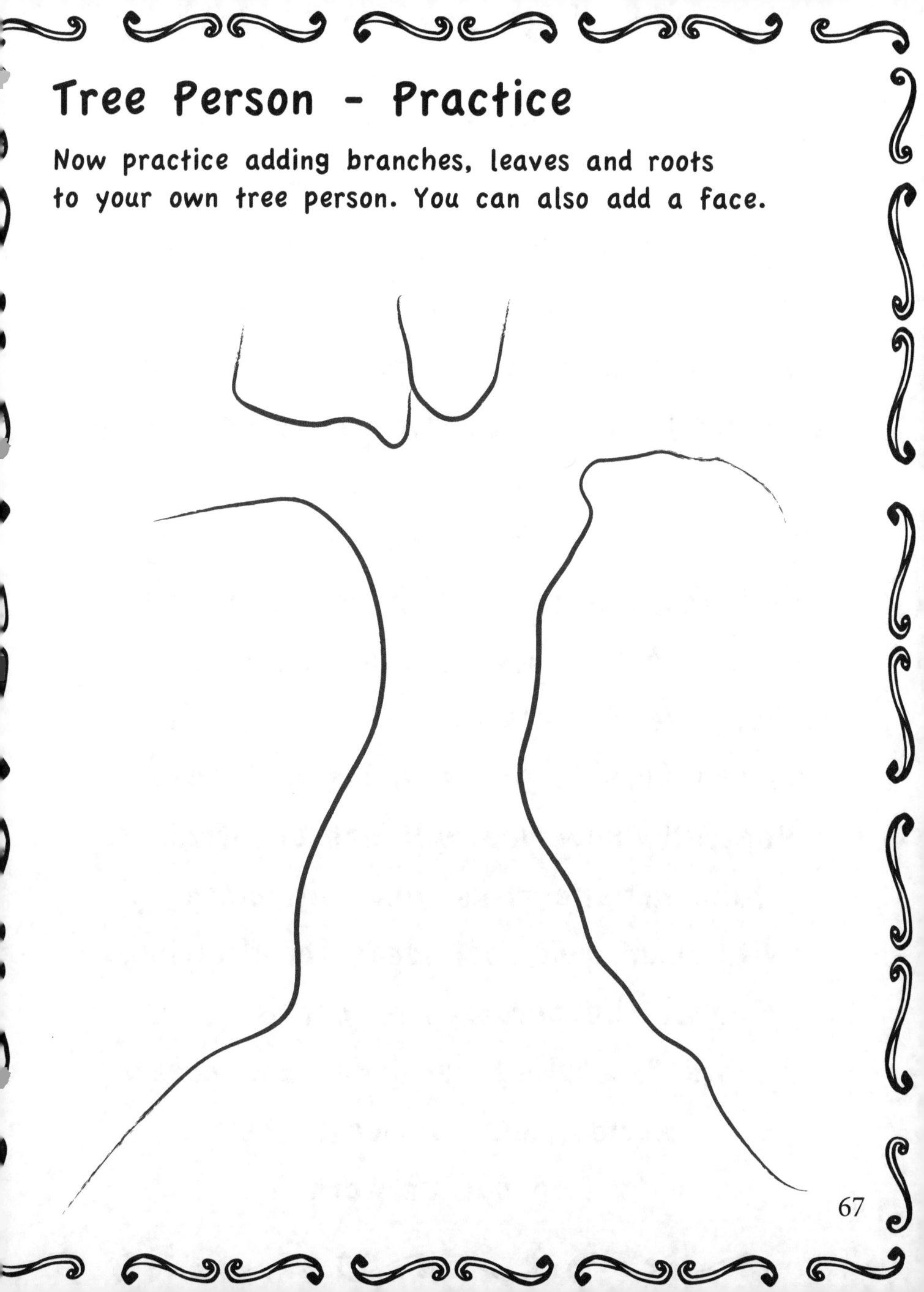

Final Note

Now that you have gone through all of the fun exercises in this book, we hope you have opened up a channel of creativity and imagination that you didn't previously know you had.

The purpose of this book was to show you that there is more than one way to look at art. Art is not always meant to be a perfect, pretty picture. Art is also interesting, thought provoking, intriguing and strange. Hopefully now you will not be afraid to take artistic risks, and will come up with your own cool ideas for drawings. One of the purposes of art is to be able to explore our inner and outer worlds, and to merge them into our artwork.

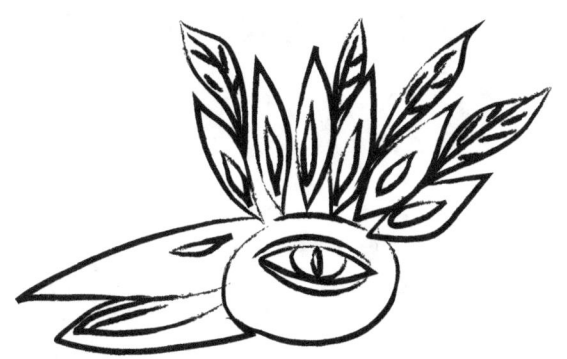

We hope you have enjoyed this book, now take the time to practice your surrealist art drawings every day!
You can use some of the pages at the back of the paperback version of this book for practice drawings, to get started.
You can also purchase yourself a few inexpensive sketchbooks and fill those up!
If you liked this book, please take a moment to leave a review on Amazon.com. Reviews help to make more great books for you to enjoy!

Thank you!

Drawing Practice Page

Drawing Practice Page

Drawing Practice Page

Drawing Practice Page

Drawing Practice Page

Drawing Practice Page

Drawing Practice Page

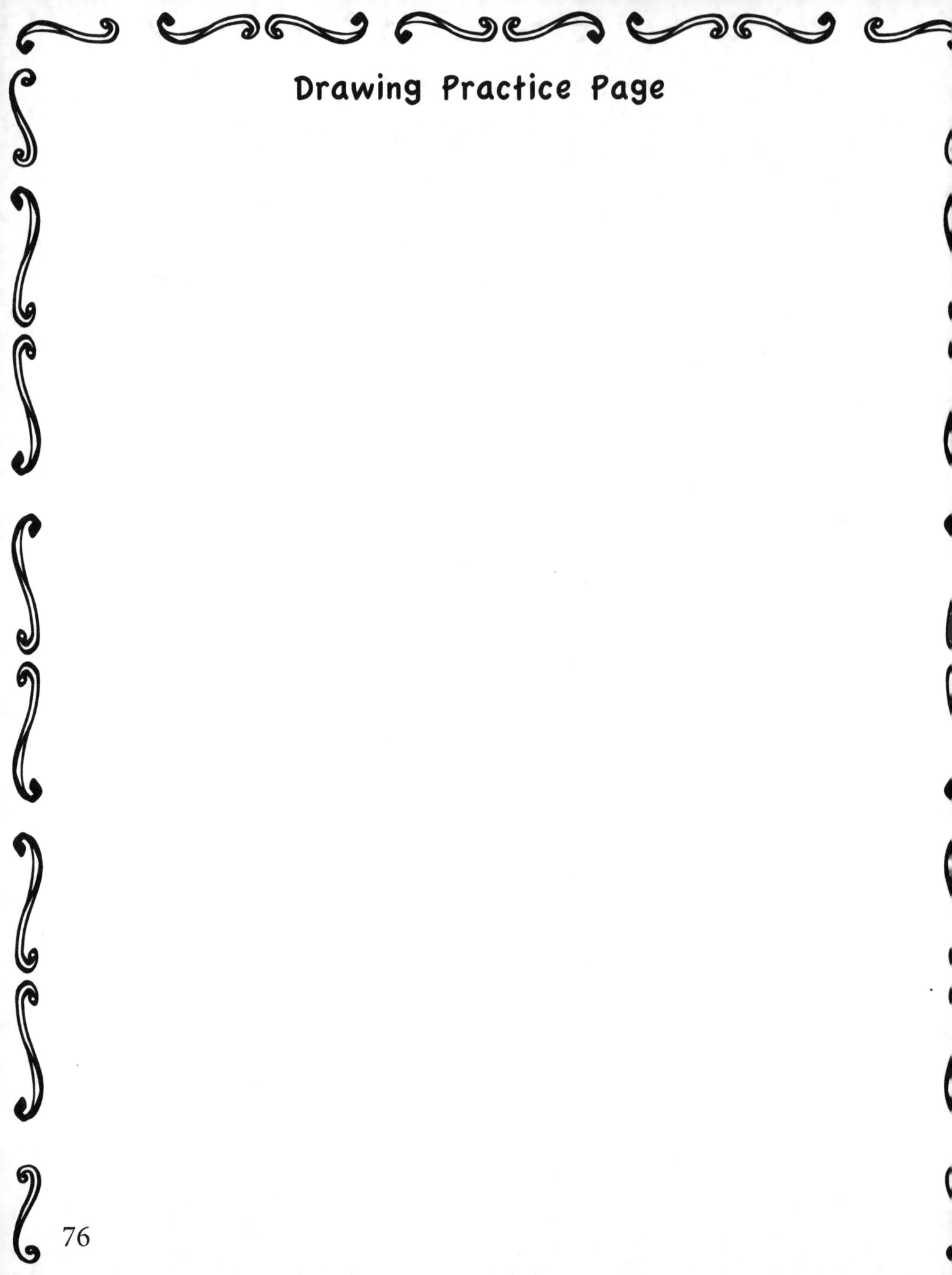

Drawing Practice Page

Drawing Practice Page

Drawing Practice Page

Drawing Practice Page

Drawing Practice Page

Drawing Practice Page

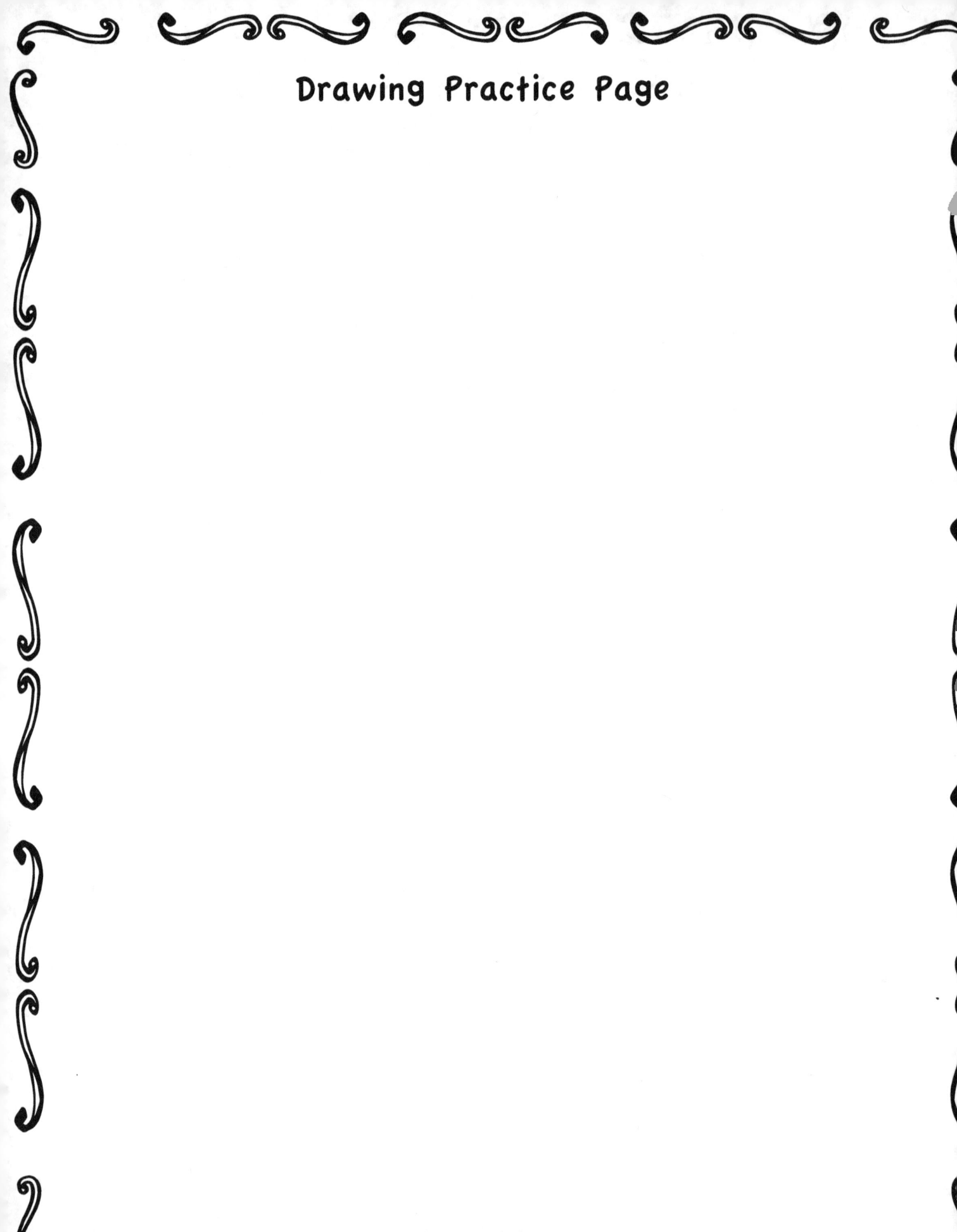

Drawing Practice Page

Drawing Practice Page

Drawing Practice Page

Drawing Practice Page

Drawing Practice Page

Drawing Practice Page

Drawing Practice Page

Drawing Practice Page

Drawing Practice Page

Drawing Practice Page

Drawing Practice Page

Drawing Practice Page

Drawing Practice Page

Drawing Practice Page

Drawing Practice Page

Drawing Practice Page

Drawing Practice Page

Drawing Practice Page